TRADITIONS OF CHRISTIAN SPIRITUALITY

BRIDES IN THE DESERT

D0862167

BRIDES IN THE DESERT

The Spirituality of the Beguines

SASKIA MURK-JANSEN

SERIES EDITOR:
Philip Sheldrake

ORBIS BOOKS

Maryknoll, New York 10545

The Catholic Foreign Mission Society of America (Maryknoll) recruits and trains people for overseas missionary service. Through Orbis Books, Maryknoll aims to foster the international dialogue that is essential to mission. The books published, however, reflect the opinions of their authors and are not meant to represent the official position of the society.

First published in 1998 by
Darton, Longman and Todd Ltd.
1 Spencer Court
140–142 Wandsworth High Street
London SW18 4JJ
Great Britain

Published in the USA in 1998 by
Orbis Books
P.O. Box 308
Maryknoll, New York 10545–0308
U.S.A.

ISBN 1–57075–201–X

Designed by Sandie Boccacci
Phototypeset in 10/13¼pt New Century Schoolbook
by Intype London Ltd
Printed and bound in Great Britain by
Redwood Books, Trowbridge, Wiltshire

Library of Congress Cataloging-in-Publication Data

Murk-Jansen, Saskia.
    Brides in the desert : the spirituality of the Beguines / Saskia
Murk-Jansen.
        p.   cm.—(Traditions of Christian spirituality)
    Includes bibliographical references and index.
    ISBN 1–57075–201–X (pbk.)
    1. Beguines. I. Title. II. Series.
BX4272.M   1998
273′.6—dc21
                                                                98–18340
                                                                CIP

CONTENTS

Acknowledgements   6
Preface by Philip Sheldrake   7
Introduction   11

1. The Origins and Development of the   15
   Beguine Movement

2. The Literary Context   34

3. Four Lives: Four Texts   59

4. The Beguines and the Church   79

5. Brides in the Desert: Key Images in   89
   Beguine Spirituality

6. Conclusion   113

   Notes   121
   Selected Bibliography   131

ACKNOWLEDGEMENTS

The writing of a book, even a modest one such as this, is the product of many years' reflection, and inevitably the work of many hands. It is alas not possible to list all those whose conversations, remarks and casual observations contributed to the gradual development of the thesis presented here. Nevertheless, I would like to acknowledge and thank the many students, colleagues and fellow conference delegates who, by their reactions, questions and comments have over the years helped me to refine my thoughts on Beguine spirituality. There are several conversations with members of the Senior Combination Room at Robinson College that I recall especially vividly as milestones along the way. None of it would have happened were it not for the personally supportive and academically challenging environment of Robinson College, so a particular vote of thanks should go to the Warden and Fellows for providing the context for my research and teaching. Thanks are also due to my husband, John Barker, who listened patiently and provided helpful advice and encouragement at many points, and special thanks to our daughter, Catherine Eleonora Joy, whose first year unfolded to the sound of her mother typing and without whose patience and forbearance this book would not have been possible.

Robinson College
University of Cambridge
April 1988

PREFACE TO THE SERIES

Nowadays, in the western world, there is a widespread hunger for spirituality in all its forms. This is not confined to traditional religious people let alone to regular churchgoers. The desire for resources to sustain the spiritual quest has led many people to seek wisdom in unfamiliar places. Some have turned to cultures other than their own. The fascination with Native American or Aboriginal Australian spiritualities is a case in point. Other people have been attracted by the religions of India and Tibet or the Jewish Kabbalah and Sufi mysticism. One problem is that, in comparison to other religions, Christianity is not always associated in people's minds with 'spirituality'. The exceptions are a few figures from the past who have achieved almost cult status such as Hildegard of Bingen or Meister Eckhart. This is a great pity for Christianity East and West over two thousand years has given birth to an immense range of spiritual wisdom. Many traditions continue to be active today. Others that were forgotten are being rediscovered and reinterpreted.

It is a long time since an extended series of introductions to Christian spiritual traditions has been available in English. Given the present climate, it is an opportune moment for a new series which will help more people to be aware of the great spiritual riches available within the Christian tradition.

The overall purpose of the series is to make selected spiritual traditions available to a contemporary readership. The books seek to provide accurate and balanced historical and thematic treatments of their subjects. The authors are also conscious of the need to make connections with contemporary experience and values without being artificial or reducing a tradition to one dimension. The authors are well-versed in reliable scholarship about the traditions they describe. However, their intention is that the books should be fresh in style and accessible to the general reader.

One problem that such a series inevitably faces is the word 'spirituality'. For example, it is increasingly used beyond religious circles and does not necessarily imply a faith tradition. Again, it could mean substantially different things for a Christian and a Buddhist. Within Christianity itself, the word in its modern sense is relatively recent. The reality that it stands for differs subtly in the different contexts of time and place. Historically, 'spirituality' covers a breadth of human experience and a wide range of values and practices.

No single definition of 'spirituality' has been imposed on the authors in this series. Yet, despite the breadth of the series there is a sense of a common core in the writers themselves and in the traditions they describe. All Christian spiritual traditions have their source in three things. First, while drawing on ordinary experience and even religious insights from elsewhere, Christian spiritualities are rooted in the scriptures and particularly in the gospels. Second, spiritual traditions are not derived from abstract theory but from attempts to live out gospel values in a positive yet critical way within specific historical and cultural contexts. Third, the experiences and insights of individuals and groups are not isolated but are related to the wider Christian tradition of beliefs, practices and community life. From a Christian perspective, spirituality is not just concerned with prayer or even with narrowly religious activities. It concerns the whole of human life, viewed in terms of a conscious relationship with God, in Jesus Christ, through the indwelling of the Holy Spirit and within a community of believers.

The series as a whole includes traditions that probably would not have appeared twenty years ago. The authors themselves have been encouraged to challenge, where appropriate, inaccurate assumptions about their particular tradition. While conscious of their own biases, authors have nonetheless sought to correct the imbalances of the past. Previous understandings of what is mainstream or 'orthodox' sometimes need to be questioned. People or practices that became marginal demand to be re-examined. Studies of spirituality in the past frequently underestimated or ignored the role of women. Sometimes the treatments of spiritual traditions were culturally one-sided because they were written from an uncritical western European or North Atlantic perspective.

However, any series is necessarily selective. It cannot hope to do full justice to the extraordinary variety of Christian spiritual traditions. The principles of selection are inevitably open to question. I hope that an appropriate balance has been maintained between a sense of the likely readership on the one hand and the dangers of narrowness on the other. In the end, choices had to be made and the result is inevitably weighted in favour of traditions that have achieved 'classic' status or which seem to capture the contemporary imagination. Within these limits, I trust that the series will offer a reasonably balanced account of what the Christian spiritual tradition has to offer.

As editor of the series I would like to thank all the authors who agreed to contribute and for the stimulating conversations and correspondence that sometimes resulted. I am especially grateful for the high quality of their work which made my task so much easier. Editing such a series is a complex undertaking. I have worked closely throughout with Morag Reeve of Darton, Longman & Todd and Robert Ellsberg of Orbis Books. I am immensely grateful to them for their friendly support and judicious advice. Without them this series would never have come together.

PHILIP SHELDRAKE
Sarum College, Salisbury

INTRODUCTION

The Beguine movement was a lay women's religious movement that arose in the early years of the thirteenth century. The Beguines did not follow any established rule, but lived lives of apostolic poverty and chastity doing works of charity among the poor and the sick. They are frequently associated with hospitals, especially leper hospitals, and with schools. The life they led, especially as they lived from the work of their hands rather than relying on charity, was heralded as the most perfect form of Christian life by leading theologians of the time. The lives they led caused the Beguines to develop a spirituality that was both in and of the world, not separated from it, which makes their texts particularly interesting for us today. The women who became Beguines in the early years were predominantly from wealthy families and the education they had enjoyed is reflected in the quality of the texts they wrote. The women whose work is discussed in this book, Beatrijs of Nazareth, Hadewijch, Mechtild of Magdeburg and Marguerite Porete, span the thirteenth century. Their work is important for several reasons. The texts are significant from the point of view of literary history as they represent some of the earliest examples of vernacular literature. The quality of the writing is also exceptional: the poetry of Hadewijch, for example, is among the best in the Dutch language of any century. From the point of view of the history of religious thought, the texts are some of the earliest and finest examples of vernacular theology. From a theological point of view their insights into the relationship between the creature and the Creator are a most valuable supplement to those available in other texts. The texts they wrote are for the most part mystical – by means of visions, poetry and prose they explore the deepest, most intimate aspects of the relationship between God and the soul. They are writing in the monastic tradition which prefers affective experience, the knowledge gained by loving, over reason. As women living largely in the world, rather than cloistered from it, they are confronted by the paradox of suffering in a world created by a loving God, and their response to this paradox is both interesting and creative.

To hear any voices from the Middle Ages clearly poses particular problems as we are divided from the Middle Ages by much more than time. Medieval voices come to us muffled by the intervening curtain of Aristotelian logic and rationalism. Since the thirteenth century we have become ever more convinced of the importance of the literal word and of discursive, rational language. We have thereby lost touch with the language of the period up to the fourteenth century – a language of images. Images are always multi-valent, open to many levels of interpretation. When you use images to speak of God, there is no pretence of absolute accuracy – nor are you limited to saying just one thing at a time. We have become so accustomed to discursive language that we are only just beginning to learn to 'read' image language once more. The Beguines with their rich and at times startling use of image and metaphor may be able to help us. For example, the problem many Christians have with the description of God as Father, fixing on it as implying the literal maleness of the Divinity, may be eased if that image is just one among many. The two stratagems for speaking about God, the apophatic (where language about God fails and all that can be said is a denial of what has been said before) and the cataphatic (a riot of language and different voices talking about God in as many conflicting ways as possible), are profoundly linked in their recognition of the fact that any image we choose to use about God can be no more than an image; it should not be regarded as a statement of fact. The more obviously inappropriate the images are the less likely they are to lure us into anthropomorphism. Equally it is in the proliferation of words about God that the inadequacy of those words is revealed.

The *mysterium tremendum* aspect of the Deity is central to the Beguines' understanding of him. They use images, metaphor and paradox in an attempt to evoke in their audience something similar to their own experiences of God. They are acutely conscious of the mysterious otherness of God, and have a sense of awe and even of horror at the enormity of the love that God has towards his creatures. Perhaps the single biblical text that best encapsulates the complexities of Beguine spirituality is Psalm 22. The terms used by the Beguines to describe the suffering experienced in their love and desire for the presence of God are reminiscent of the Psalmist's description: 'I am poured out like water, and all my bones are out of joint: my heart is like wax' (Psalm 22:14). It is their experience that within the desperation and suffering of the cry of Jesus on the cross, 'My God, my God why hast thou forsaken me?' (Psalm 22:1), is contained the seed of the certainty that 'when he cried unto him he heard' (Psalm 22:24). The Beguines recognise that it is precisely at that moment of agony of longing love that (wo)man is closest to God. In the twentieth century we have somewhat lost the awareness of the numinous, of the (W)Holy Other, in the desire to emphasise the accessibility and humanity of Jesus. It may be time for the pendulum to begin to swing back. The Beguines articulate what many have felt, namely the wonder at the love that is God while trembling in fear and awe at the gulf that separates Creator from creature. By reacquainting ourselves with ways of dealing with the numinous, guided by those who have gone before us, we may find new ways of talking about God.

To read texts of the past today, whether for spiritual guidance or not, demands of the reader one of two approaches. Readers can simply ignore any elements that appear strange or inapplicable to the contemporary situation. Alternatively, they need to be prepared to put some effort into learning about the context in which the author was writing, thereby making the strange seem at least comprehensible, and possibly seeing unexpected applications today of that which seemed strange before. To appreciate the voices of the Beguines, it is necessary to spend time acquainting oneself with their context. For this reason there are several chapters devoted to a discussion of the social, historical, literary and theological context of the Beguines, as well as those dealing more directly with the texts themselves. It is in the specificity and particular details of their social and historical context that the subtlety of their teachings are revealed. To read them without an understanding of the context in which they wrote is to risk interpreting them according to a late-twentieth-century agenda, and overlooking the very elements that make them special. The study of texts such as these can be a tremendous source of inspiration and strength to us today. The extra work involved in seeking to understand the context in which the authors were writing is amply rewarded by the dawning realisation that a common bond links all those who seek earnestly to draw nearer to God.

1. THE ORIGINS AND DEVELOPMENT OF THE BEGUINE MOVEMENT

The Beguines were a lay women's movement that started in the thirteenth century. This was a period of religious revival characterised by a widespread desire to live close to the apostolic ideal in poverty, chastity and service to others in the face of the increasing materialism of the age. Like the Franciscans and Dominicans, both also founded in the first quarter of the thirteenth century, Beguines were an urban phenomenon. The thirteenth century was a period of social change and increasing urbanisation in northern Europe, the towns rapidly became the centres of population and of increasing commercial activity, and it is against this background that the great upsurge of popular piety, of religious movements seeking to emulate apostolic poverty, should be seen. As well as the mendicant orders sanctioned by the Church, others such as the Humiliati and the Waldensians, whose interpretation of Scripture brought them into conflict with the Church, were active in the cities. Much of the religious debate took the shape of lively preaching and good preachers attracted large audiences. These audiences included a substantial proportion of women, and the immediacy and urgency of religious debate inspired and fuelled the expression of popular feminine piety. Unlike the Franciscans and the Dominicans, the Beguines sought to live the apostolic life without being members of any recognised order, and the lay nature of the movement almost brought its downfall within a hundred years of its inception. However, as the many lovely beguinages in modern Belgium dating from later centuries testify, the movement survived and continued, although in a slightly modified form, to the present day.

Because Beguines followed no authorised rule, the details of their lives varied considerably according to where and when they lived. Some women were able to live as Beguines within their families, others lived together in small or large groups, though as the thirteenth century progressed the larger communities became the norm.

The thirteenth century was a period of major change and intellectual adjustment. The total sum of knowledge and skill increased dramatically in a relatively short time, with consequent changes in mental attitudes. The Pisan Leonardo Fibonacci is credited with introducing the use of Arabic numerals to the West in 1202, in particular that critical innovation the number 0. The consequent greater ease of notation and computation, as well as the influence of other branches of mathematics such as algebra, encouraged an increasingly accurate numerical conception of the world. The growth in mathematical mentality produced unexpected advances in technology. The construction of Gothic buildings such as the glorious Sainte Chapelle, for example, built for the French king St Louis between 1243 and 1248, required an elaborate understanding of geometry and arithmetic. The calculation of interest was made simpler, stimulating investment by bankers in trade.[1] The development at the end of the twelfth century of the keel and rudder and of the compass also encouraged a growth in trade outside the Mediterranean and coastal waters. Trading interests prompted the journeys to China of the Polos, and their discovery of peoples ignorant of the Bible in turn stimulated the missionary activity of the medieval Church.[2]

Trade was the main source of wealth and social mobility during the thirteenth century. The concentration of the previously largely rural population in urban centres encouraged trade and commerce.[3] The developing urban society was more mixed in terms of its members' origins than society had been previously. It was dominated by the principle of achievement, achievement measured by wealth and ostentation. The sharp differences of wealth and social prestige within the towns were emphasised by the numerous occasions for elaborate display, such as religious festivals, and many municipal councils were eventually to find themselves obliged to legislate against luxury.[4] The increasing interest in earthly goods can also be seen in the development of legal concepts of property, and the way in which avarice began to take precedence over pride in the list of deadly sins.[5]

The Church did not escape the increasing materialism of urban life, and this prompted calls for its further reform and a return to the apostolic purity of the early Church. The striving for purity of religious life also fuelled the development of heretical movements including that known variously as the Cathar or Albigensian heresy which spread quickly across much of Europe. These movements proved particularly attractive to women as they offered them the opportunity to live more spiritual lives. Large numbers of orthodox women also sought to live lives of apostolic poverty, and the Church was to see in them both a potential threat and a possible weapon against the spread of heresy. The twelfth century had seen a great upsurge of religious feeling among the laity, especially women, and by the thirteenth century existing orders were no longer able or willing to absorb the large numbers of women wishing to live lives of chastity and poverty and service to the poor. The religious revival of the twelfth and thirteenth centuries was a development of the movement that spurred the Gregorian reforms of the eleventh century.[6] In order to strengthen the hierarchical structure of the Church which was based on the apostolic succession,[7] Pope Gregory VII held that only worthy priests could validly perform religious functions and had unchaste priests, as well as those who owed their office to simony, pursued as heretics. Once the idea of the 'worthiness of the priest' had penetrated the consciousness of the laity it proved hard to eradicate. Many began to ask whether anyone ordained by the Church but whose life was not modelled on that of the apostles could be a true priest. A religious consciousness arose which saw Christianity as a way of life laid down in the Gospels which was binding on all genuine Christians. The linked concepts of evangelical poverty and the desire for apostolic life and work became the joint focus of a new conception of the essence of Christianity which is reflected in the religious movements of the following century.

In response to the Gregorian reforms, a number of new orders came into existence early in the twelfth century, all of which reflected similar preoccupations but satisfied rather different needs: the Cistercians, the Augustinian Canons and the Premonstratensian Order or White Canons.[8]

The *Cistercians* were formed as a more rigorous branch of the Benedictine Order – Cîteaux, founded in 1098, sought to revive the primitive rule of St Benedict. Their churches were relatively unadorned and the monks adhered strictly to the full order of service, singing the whole Psalter every month. Unlike the Benedictines, the Cistercian Order did not accept child oblates (children given to God by their parents often at a very early age to live their entire lives in the monastery) and their way of life was deliberately hard. They settled by preference in remote frontier country or wilderness areas, considerable tracts of which remained around Europe at this period. By settling these areas the Order performed a very useful function, colonising the country.[9] Not surprisingly they had great strength in the Iberian Peninsula where Cistercian monasteries followed closely the conquering Christian armies as they strove to drive back the Moors. In order to cultivate and work the wild land they chose to settle on, the Order used lay brothers, called 'conversi'. These men were illiterate, at least in the sense of reading no Latin, and were forbidden to aspire to full monastic status which required the ability to read Latin. Nevertheless, in this use of lay brothers the Cistercians were the first to offer a full assurance of salvation to illiterates – though at this stage only to men, not women.[10]

Probably the single most influential Cistercian was Bernard of Clairvaux. He joined Cîteaux not long after its foundation in 1112, initially against family opposition. In this he is a forerunner of later movements in that he took with him into the monastery a large number of his relatives and friends, including married men who left wives and children. In 1115 he was sent to found the new Cistercian house at Clairvaux and eventually died there in 1153. Bernard is the great exponent of monastic theology, a theological discourse drawing on experience and using images and allegory for its expression. His Sermons on the Song of Songs were very influential on the language and images of mystics in northern Europe.

The *Augustinians* sought to go even further back than the Cistercians and wished to revive primitive biblical Christianity. They found their rule in a letter of St Augustine, hence their name. Interestingly for an entirely male order, the letter was in fact addressed to a group of women.[11] Where the Cistercians sought to serve society by praying for it at a distance, the Augustinian Canons aimed to serve society by performing acts of charity. They therefore settled in the vicinity of towns and castles. The development of this order coincides with evidence of an increasing interest in and concern for the poor as individuals, not simply as an opportunity for alms giving for the rich.[12] In this desire to live the apostolic ideal and to serve the people by bringing God closer to society, the Augustinians are the precursors of the mendicant orders of the next century.

The *Premonstratensians* were founded by Norbert of Xanten in 1120. Although he ended his life as Archbishop of Magdeburg, Norbert of Xanten began his religious career as an itinerant preacher in Flanders. The large numbers of itinerant preachers, or *Wanderprediger* as they have become known, were a significant feature of twelfth-century religious life. These men travelled from town to town preaching in market places and fields as they went. Their theme was corruption in the Church and the need for reform. (It has been argued that the reforms which swept the Church in this period were in fact a response to the increasingly vociferous demands from the people as illustrated by the tremendous followings enjoyed by these itinerant preachers.) Some preachers went too far in their critique of the Church and were judged heretical, but many more went on to enjoy honoured positions within the Church surrounded by the odour of sanctity.[13]

The crowds that flocked to hear the preachers were drawn from all ranks of society, and as they travelled the preachers gathered large numbers of enthusiastic followers who travelled with them from place to place. Not all of these followers were men, indeed a large proportion of them were women. Robert of Arbrissal at the end of the eleventh century was forced to found a convent at Fontevrault in order to house and care for the many women who followed him from town to town to hear him preach. Initially the social composition of this foundation was varied, reflecting the crowds of women who followed him. However, within a short period of time, it became very aristocratic. It was the burial place of the counts of Anjou and the refuge of the women of the greatest families of northern France, including Eleanor Queen of England. Norbert too attracted a large following of women and he founded the Order at Premontre in order to provide these women with an outlet for their religious fervour. In the early years of the Order a number of double monasteries were founded but by the end of the century the Order had closed its doors to women.[14]

The Order followed the Augustinian Rule, but a number of supplementary statutes made their life even more austere. Norbert was a friend and admirer of Bernard of Clairvaux so it is not surprising that the Order shows a blending of Augustinian and Cistercian ideals. The monasteries were founded in the vicinity of towns and particular emphasis was laid on preaching and the care of souls. Nevertheless the Order also came to play an important part in the conversion and colonisation of the lands east of the Elbe after their founder was made Archbishop of Magdeburg in 1126, in much the same way that the Cistercians did in Iberia.[15]

These new religious foundations gave men the possibility of living according to the religious ideals, but few such opportunities were available for women. During the twelfth century existing opportunities were put under ever greater strain by the increasing demand. As we have seen, some convents were founded specifically to meet the need, such as that at Fontevrault, and the Premonstratensian Order was in part established to satisfy the demand. By mid-century the Cistercians, too, could no longer ignore the existence of women. Convents were established, especially in Spain where there were some notably large foundations, but they were not officially mentioned until 1191. These convents were inevitably dependent on monasteries in their vicinity, and because of their size and growth the monasteries concerned soon felt that they were too much of a burden. Their existence was officially acknowledged only for it to be declared that no more convents were to be established, and no new nuns were to be accepted by those that already existed. By the end of the century, therefore, these opportunities which had briefly opened up for women to live a religious life within the Church were rapidly closing again: Fontevrault had become such an élite aristocratic institution as to be inaccessible to all but a few; the Premonstratensian Order had abandoned the ideal of double monasteries and had closed its doors to women; and the Cistercian Order, which had been admitting women almost by accident, had called a halt to this unwelcome expansion. That the established orders were not immediately successful in implementing these decisions appears from the number of apparently conclusive statements and decrees issued by the governing bodies of both the Premonstratensian and Cistercian Orders in successive years banning women from joining the orders. This then was the scene at the start of the thirteenth century. While the main orders were becoming increasingly strident in their efforts to close their doors to women, there were ever increasing numbers of men and women seeking to live a religious life of apostolic poverty and service in the cities.

The apparently huge numbers of women flocking to the Church at this period has given rise to what has become known as the *Frauenfrage*, the 'woman-question'. The question has three main elements: why were women attracted to the religious life? What kind of women were they? And why were there so many of them? A frequently voiced theory is that the women attracted to the religious life were only the poor and unmarriageable who had no other options open to them, or those terrified of childbirth. The theory seems to have originated in the research by Karl Bücher on a beguinage for poor Beguines towards the end of the fourteenth century and in the fifteenth century, and is arguably less relevant to the early years of the movement.[16] Scholars have sought to explain the numbers by positing a sudden increase in the number of women, or in the longevity of women, and consequently a scarcity of available men. The increased numbers of women has been attributed on the one hand to fewer conflicts in which they were killed or taken prisoner, and on the other to an increased level of iron in the diet leading to fewer deaths in childbirth. The former seems to overlook the fact that fewer conflicts would also result in fewer men being killed, so that the two might go some way towards cancelling each other out. The latter attributes the increased iron in the diet to an increase of legumes in the diet, and the use of iron cooking pots.

Such theories have the appeal of neatness, but they are unfortunately not wholly supported by the available facts. The suggestion that the women drawn to the religious life did so from personal necessity being overwhelmingly poor and unmarriageable, or frightened of childbirth, is hard to prove or disprove. The poor leave few traces in historical records, so that the absence of information about poor women joining the Beguines is scarcely conclusive. Nevertheless, Grundmann has shown that all the evidence we do have on women who joined the Beguines points conclusively in the opposite direction – to wealthy women of the nobility and especially of the newly emerging urban patriciate, many of them married or rejecting advantageous offers of marriage. The numerous different rules for beguinages also imply that the women joining them had property of a more or less substantial kind.[17] Indeed it could be argued that many of the rules effectively excluded the poor from becoming Beguines. Some of the women choosing the religious life in preference to marriage may have done so out of fear for the consequences, but many of those who became Beguines were mothers already.

That there was, in the course of the first millennium after the birth of Christ, an increase in the longevity of women is uncontroversial. The increase however was gradual and never sufficiently large within one or two generations to explain an entire religious movement. An increase in legumes in the diet will have helped reduce anaemia in the population and therefore also in childbearing women. It is known that such an increase occurred following the invention of the horse collar in the late ninth or early tenth century. This, together with the invention of the horse shoe and tandem harness, enabled larger fields to be placed under cultivation with deeper ploughs.[18] It is also true that by the thirteenth century iron cooking pots were coming into use. However, they are unlikely to have been very widely used. Even in the fourteenth century John of Gaunt's register shows iron cooking pots to have been a considerable item of expenditure. Even if they had been more widely used, it is hard to see how the use of such pots could have reduced iron deficiency in women, since iron in the form of iron filings or iron oxide (commonly known as rust) cannot normally be absorbed by the body. This however leaves the central question of the 'Frauenfrage' unanswered: why did so many women wish to enter religious life at this time? Perhaps the answer must be sought not in the numbers but in their motivation. The success of the two mendicant orders and the heresies they were founded to combat show how the new conception of Christianity as a way of life rather than a collection of dogmas, and the understanding that the gospel's demands were relevant, not only to those ordained by the Church but to everyone including women, inspired many to change their way of life. The growth of the Beguine movement is another example of the same phenomenon.

The Beguine movement is generally held to have started with the papal dispensation obtained in 1215 by Jacques of Vitry from the newly elected Pope Honorious III for women living together in chastity and poverty, doing works of

Christian charity to do so unmolested and to be able to exhort one another to increased piety and good works. Jacques of Vitry had intended to ask the dispensation from Innocent III who was known for his sympathetic support for the new forms of religious life emerging at that time.[19] However, when he arrived in Rome it was to learn that Innocent had just died, so he had to await the election of the next pope. Fortunately the new pope was minded to carry on the policies of his predecessor, as we certainly have the dispensation to these women to exhort one another to greater piety to thank for the remarkable flowering of spiritual writing in the vernaculars during the century that followed.

Jacques of Vitry had studied in Paris, possibly under Peter Cantor, and obtained his masters degree. Some time around 1211, he came to Oignies near Liege from Paris, attracted by the reputation of a holy woman, Marie d'Oignies. She was born in 1177 and died in 1213 aged 36 after a short illness. Jacques of Vitry wrote the *vita*, which is how we know of her, two years after her death in 1215. She had been married at fourteen but soon she persuaded her husband that they should give all their goods to the poor and live a life of chastity, caring for lepers. Several years later, Marie, with the agreement of her husband, left him and settled in a community of women in the vicinity of a house of Augustinian Canons. It is clear from the *vita* that Jacques was deeply impressed by Marie, by her piety and her lifestyle. He appears to have respected her for her powerful personality as well as for her unusual gifts. He had the reputation of being one of the most fluent and persuasive vernacular preachers of his day, and it is an indication of the respect with which he wishes his readers to view Marie that he ascribes his ability to preach to her influence. He describes how she persuades him to preach in the vernacular and enables him to do so by praying for him as he speaks. It was only in contact with the spirituality of Marie, sent by God to act as her voice, that he was able to develop the skill for which he became famous. Whether or not this was the literal truth is less important than the fact that this famous preacher thought it important to present the relationship in this light. By 1213 his reputation as a preacher in the vernacular prompted the Pope to invite him to preach the Albigensian crusade.

When Jacques of Vitry wrote his life of Marie d'Oignies in 1215 he did so with a polemical purpose in mind, namely the fight against the Albigensian heresy which similarly inspired the formation of the Dominicans. The Albigensians, with their *perfecti*, the 'perfect ones' who abstained from sexual relations and lived lives of ascetic purity and devotion, attracted many followers on account of the rigour and purity of their lives in perceived contrast with those of many of the clergy of the established Church. The life of Marie d'Oignies was written to be a shining example of the fact that it was possible to be holy, devout and pure even within the Catholic Church. The benefit of multiplying such examples will not have been lost on the Pope when Jacques of Vitry sought his dispensation for the women who would become known as Beguines.[20]

Marie herself was clearly not the first Beguine. The *vita* describes her joining an already established community of women attached to a house of Augustinian Canons. The Beguines – living lives of apostolic poverty and chastity, dedicated to works of Christian charity but without taking the vows of an established order – were probably a development from the unenclosed lay sisters of orders such as the Cistercians and Premonstratensians. An analysis of the lives of notable Premonstratensian sisters shows that even the enclosed choir nuns were not in fact strictly enclosed and frequently had charge of the hospital. The lay sisters of the Order principally worked among the poor and infirm and were engaged in useful tasks within the wider community.[21]

Within ten years of Jacques of Vitry obtaining papal dispensation for their irregular way of life, that way of life had been extolled by such influential figures as Robert Grosseteste and the Parisian theologian Robert of Sorbonne. What especially attracted the admiration of these men was the fact that the women, unlike other orders, did not beg or live on charity, rather they sought to live from the work of their hands. However, as was the case with other movements active against heresies accepted by the Church, the name Beguine was used indiscriminately for orthodox as well as heretical groups,[22] and in the course of the century the odour of sanctity surrounding the Beguines began to turn sour. The similarities between their way of life and that of the Cathars which the Church had emphasised in the battle against heresy, all too easily laid the women open to accusations of heresy themselves. A woman who refused a priest's sexual advances, thereby implicitly criticising the moral standards of the Church and placing herself above them, was relatively easy to accuse of the Albigensian heresy. Grundmann has shown that a number of women paid the ultimate penalty for saying no.[23] How many more preferred instead to turn that no into a yes is impossible to guess. Some will have done so, and it is ironic that within a very few years Beguines were being accused of a different heresy, that of the Free Spirit, one of the key features of which (if the confessions extracted under torture are to be believed) was extreme sexual licence.[24]

The precise origins of the name Beguine are obscure. Even in the thirteenth century there were several different theories as to the word's derivation. Matthew of Paris, otherwise a reliable and knowledgeable source of information, remarks that the reason for the use of the term is unknown. Some commentators, including the authors of rules for beguinages, claimed that it was derived from the name of a supposed 'founder' of the Beguine movement, variously identified as Lambert le Begue or Jehans li Beguins (probably Jean de Nivelles), both from Liege. Some chroniclers use the word to refer to adherents of the Albigensian heresy. Others, perhaps in an attempt to give the word a more sympathetic etymology, suggest that the word comes from the Latin *benignitate*, or because the women burn with pious zeal *'quasi bono igne ignitae'*. What is certain is that Beguines started to use the word themselves around the middle of the thirteenth century, by which time presumably any pejorative meaning it may have had had faded. It is now generally accepted that the word derives from Albigensian and that it was used indiscriminately of orthodox and heretical groups of lay women whose way of life had similar characteristics.[25]

The large and beautiful beguinages in Belgium give a false impression of the early years of the movement. One of the characteristics of the Beguine movement is that there was no founder, no single rule, no agreed way of life. Not only did beguinages change considerably over time, they were also very different in different places. The fact that a rule exists for a beguinage in Strasbourg for example really gives us no clue as to the way a Beguine might have lived in Antwerp or Magdeburg. The extant rules must therefore be seen only as examples of ways of life that were followed under the general title of Beguine, not in any way typical for other houses in other locations or at other times.[26] Initially Beguines lived alone or in small groups of perhaps half a dozen like-minded women. Those living alone might do so surrounded by their families. Small groups would gather around a woman of a particularly high reputation and might live in a house belonging to one of them. An interesting example is that of Elizabeth of Thuringia's harp player Alheid who left her mistress's entourage in Nuremberg in 1211 to live a life of penance and dedicated to the love of God. Not long afterwards, a small community of pious women asked her to join them and to become their mistress.[27] Only as the century wore on did these informal groups increase in size and begin to resemble the convents many of them eventually became. As they became more established their rules began to stipulate that although a Beguine was free to leave the community at any time, she could not take with her the property she had brought into it. In the early days, leaving the beguinage to re-enter the world was seen as an option; later the only reason for leaving the beguinage recognised in the rules was to enter an established order. When a group of Beguines came to live together, the women generally chose to settle in the vicinity of churches or existing religious houses. The pattern was early established by groups of women such as those near the Augustinian house that Marie d'Oignies joined. They chose to live in towns and cities near established houses of Augustinians, Premonstratensians and, later, Dominicans and Franciscans.

As the Dominicans became established in northern Europe, Beguines increasingly turned to them for spiritual guidance, and the respect accorded to the Dominicans by Beguines can be traced in many of their works. However, this was a cause of friction between the Order and the established clergy, especially in those cases where the choice of confessor was linked to the supposed unworthiness of the parish priest. The Order perceived the need to care for Beguines and other houses of women as diverting their members from the actual mission of the Order, which was preaching. It was therefore extremely reluctant to take upon itself the responsibility of the large numbers of women's houses, and on more than one occasion forbade any of its members to have anything to do with them.[28] Individual friars on the other hand appear to have welcomed the contact with the women. The interchange between them and the theologically trained Dominicans proved very fruitful for them both,[29] and in time many houses of Beguines became Dominican convents. The rapid spread of ideas, imagery and language from one area of Europe to another at this period is not a little due to the influence of the Dominicans as they travelled from city to city.

However, around the middle of the thirteenth century public opinion about the Beguines began to change. At first the women's movement distinguished itself from superficially similar heretical movements by not engaging in apostolic activity and by not insisting that the clergy and the Church maintain lives of apostolic poverty and purity in order to be found worthy of administering the sacraments. However, by the middle of the century Beguines were increasingly at the forefront of those criticising the clergy, claiming to be able to tell if a priest had committed a sexual transgression before celebrating the eucharist for example, and as the first condemnation of Marguerite Porete shows, they were beginning to preach outside their own communities as well. As early as 1274 Gilbert van Doornik reported to the Council of Lyons the *scandalum* that ignorant Beguines were reading and explaining Bible texts. The description of the Beguines as ignorant referred to their lack of a clerical education – the scandal was that they as women should dare to do so, not that they had not been properly trained. The Church was becoming increasingly uneasy at the intellectual and theological activity of the Beguines. In his *Summae quaestionum ordinarium* Henry of Ghent expressly condemns the idea of instructing women in theology or knowledge of the Bible 'on account of the weakness of their intellect' which could lead them into error.

Furthermore, whereas at the beginning of the century Beguines were being extolled for seeking to live off the work of their hands and not begging alms, it is clear that before too long many able-bodied and active Beguines were asking for alms in preference to working. The gradual change in public opinion therefore appears to have had a basis in fact, but there can be no doubt that it was eagerly fuelled and encouraged by one man, William of St Amour. A staunch defender of the ecclesiastical hierarchy and the status quo, he was very much opposed to the creation of new orders and at first he had expended much energy arguing against the newly formed Franciscan and Dominican Orders, seeking to discredit them. When, however, it became clear that the opinion of the Church was immovably against him, that the new orders enjoyed the high opinion of successive popes and that his opposition to them was likely to do him more harm than them, he switched his attention to the Beguines. Here his efforts to discredit the movement were much more successful. He drew on principles of ecclesiastical law to declare that, as laity, Beguines could not live as though they were members of a monastic order, wearing a distinctive habit and cutting their hair. Any who did so deserved excommunication. However, this was just the legalistic background for a much more wide-ranging attack on the Beguines' youth (and hence their inability to keep an oath of chastity without strict discipline), on their begging for alms although quite able to work, on their pride in voluntary poverty, and on their association with Dominicans who were usurping the rights of the established clergy. Although much of William's polemic against the Beguines can be attributed to his dislike of the new forms of religious life, others less prejudiced also began to condemn the Beguines. The tendency to use the same term for all groups of women with a superficially similar lifestyle, whether orthodox or not, will not have helped good Beguines to distinguish themselves from others who were abusing the privileges of their excellent reputation.

In June 1310 the Beguine Marguerite Porete was burned at the stake for disseminating her work *Le Mirouer des Simples Ames* (The Mirror of Simple Souls) and two years later the same articles that had been used to prove her guilty of heresy were used by the Church at the Council of Vienne to condemn the whole Beguine movement as heretical. However, it is doubtful whether the Church intended to crush the movement as the Council included a clause specifically excepting all pious women and Beguines who were not heretics: 'In saying this we by no means intend to forbid any faithful women from living as the Lord shall inspire them, provided they wish to live a life of penance and to serve God in humility, even if they have taken no vow of chastity, but live chastely together in their lodgings.'[30] The execution of Marguerite Porete and the Council of Vienne were followed in 1329 by the posthumous condemnation of the Dominican Provincial Meister Eckhart. The heresy trials of Marguerite Porete and of Eckhart focused especially on the fact that they had spoken in the vernacular of matters too profound for the laity to comprehend. The combined effect of these three events was to stifle the remarkable outpouring of vernacular writing on matters theological which characterises the thirteenth century.

As the many beautiful beguinages around Belgium which date from a rather later period than that under discussion here show, this was not the end of the movement. In France, where beguinages were never as numerous or as large as in Belgium, the Netherlands or Germany, the condemnation resulted in the rapid decline of the movement and the transfer of many beguinages to the Franciscan or Dominican ter-tiaries.[31] In Germany, too, many of the beguinages formalised their association with the mendicant orders. In the Low Count-ries, however, they continued to attract wealthy and aristocratic patrons up until the Reformation. Although most of the women who became Beguines in later periods were from more humble backgrounds than those who had started the movement, they continued the tradition of charitable works and the care of the sick. In common with the established religious orders, the level of education in the beguinages diminished and Beguines never again produced the quality of theological writing that they had done in the thirteenth century. Nevertheless, the movement continued in one form or another right up to the present day.[32]

BEGUINES IN THE BRITISH ISLES[33]

The Beguines were almost exclusively a movement of main-land Europe. There, as we have seen, they were strongest along the Rhine, in Germany and in Flanders, and less strong in France. The movement never had the same kind of fol-lowing in the British Isles, possibly because, through the influence of the Celtic Church, there was a strong tradition of hermits and recluses in these islands. However, it is thought that there may have been Beguines in East Anglia, particu-larly in Norwich. Norwich is best known for its fifteenth-century anchoress, Julian, but in addition to a number of anchoresses there were also informal religious communities of women in that city up until the sixteenth century. These informal religious communities appear to have been unique to East Anglia. In view of the extensive trade links between this part of England and Flanders it seems likely that, here as elsewhere, ideas travelled along the same routes as trade. Interesting in this context is the fact that one such informal group of women is known to have lived in a property belonging to one John Asger, a merchant born in the Low Countries.[34]

The exact nature of these informal groups is unclear. Women who wished to live a religious life seem to have gathered together to do so as a community. These groups do not appear to have been recognised officially by the Church, but they were clearly supported by the local clergy. The main evidence for their existence comes from wills. Gifts to these informal groups of women are listed with those to other religious institutions, indicating that the testators viewed the groups as primarily religious communities. They are described in terms such as 'sisters dedicated to chastity', *mulieres pauperculae* (poor women), and *sorores commerantae* (sisters living together). That the women were remembered in wills suggests that these groups had some kind of public profile, possibly through caring for the sick or helping the poor. In all these respects, the informality and lack of definite rule, the names by which they were known, and their charitable work, they closely resemble the Beguines of mainland Europe. What is not clear is the social background of the women who made up these groups. As we have seen, the early Beguines were predominantly from wealthy if not aristocratic families and as a result many of the beguinages were relatively well off. Their connections also helped ensure a continued tradition of generous patronage from aristocratic and patrician circles. However, by the sixteenth century most Beguines were from more humble backgrounds. Since the Norwich evidence is all from the later period, it seems likely that these women will have been so too.

It has been suggested that the informal groups of women in Norwich may in fact have resembled the *maisons dieu* of other medieval English cities more closely than they resembled the Beguines.[35] These were also informal, flexible, though frequently short-lived religious communities. The major difference between these houses and the beguinages of mainland Europe appears to have been that they were largely occupied by the poor, which may explain their transient nature. The greater stability of the beguinages in the Low Countries is due in part to their wealthy and later aristocratic connections. That similar informal groups of religious women did not attract similar patronage in the British Isles may have more to do with the patterns of patronage than with the lives they led or their religious motivation. As we have seen, the term Beguine was applied to a wide range of different types of communities across Europe, some of which may also have resembled the *maisons dieu*. Unfortunately it does not appear possible to reconstruct the kind of community that existed in Norwich beyond noting that here too opportunities existed for women to live together in poverty, chastity and service to others outside the formal structures of the Church.

2. THE LITERARY CONTEXT

The thirteenth century saw a remarkable flowering of theological writing in vernaculars across Europe. Made possible by the papacy's support of the Beguines, it came to a virtual end when the Church withdrew its support at the end of the century, first implicitly then explicitly at the Council of Vienne in 1312. By sanctioning the mutual encouragement and exhortation to greater virtue of lay women, the Church opened theological discussion to people previously excluded, namely women and the laity. As we have seen, this coincided with the growing perception of Christianity as a way of life that made demands on everyone not just the religious, which helps to explain the vigour and enthusiasm evident in the texts that survive. The Beguines wrote about the numinous aspect of God, which is non-rational to the extent that it is far beyond the human mind to grasp and comprehend, from their experience of him as the (W)Holy Other. Their spirituality is not rooted in theorising or speculation. Their texts contain no elaborate constructions of philosophical theories or doctrine. Faced with the numinous they sought to awaken the sense of the numinous in others. This sense cannot be taught, like doctrine or philosophical theory, it can only be evoked by awakening the latent consciousness of the numinous in (wo)man. One of the important features of Beguine writing is therefore their use of paradox, metaphor and image language, all of which are affective, unlike the discursive language of systematic theology which relies on rational explanation.

The dominance of reason in religious discourse began with the adoption of Aristotelian in preference to Platonic philosophy as the underlying context of religious thinking. Aristotle stressed the faculty of human reason and, influenced by his philosophy, Aquinas began applying reason to religion. The influence of Aristotle in the following centuries and the dominance of Thomist theology in the nineteenth century has meant that the non-rational has been ignored or brushed aside as somehow second rate. It is hardly surprising that the theological writing of the Beguines, concentrating as it does on the non-rational or supra-rational aspect of the human relationship with God, should have been forgotten as well. History always tends to be the story of the winners, of those who succeeded in getting their ideas across, and the history of spirituality is no exception.[1] Individuals are seen as significant only in retrospect because the consequences of their actions support the traditional self-image of the establishment. The desire of those in power to reinforce the structures of authority and institutions which give them their power has meant that the history of spirituality has been viewed and recorded according to the extent to which it conformed to the centre and to traditional orthodoxy. The fact that conformity is valued over pluralism means that a universal culture is valued over local or particular experience and this has made those who did not fit in even more invisible. One example of this is the dominance of male experience over female, the fact that male experience is seen as normative. To be considered important or significant a person must be presented within the accepted cultural framework. That framework is created and maintained by men, so naturally male figures fit more comfortably within it than do female ones.[2] The lives of significant spiritual female figures tend to be recorded selectively for institutional purposes so as not to disturb time-honoured patterns of attitude and behaviour.[3] The distrust of mystic literature of those scholars working on these texts has further contributed to the fact that the importance of the Beguines as creative writers and mystics has been emphasised while their theology and their stature as spiritual thinkers have been left to one side.

To modern eyes much of the Beguines' work appears to be

intensely personal, but it is important to remember that it is above all didactic literature. The women were writing to teach others and the texts were intended as spiritual guidance for their communities. In view of the Church's reputation for antagonism to women as teachers, it is reasonable to ask how the Beguines justified to themselves and to others the teaching role they took upon themselves to a greater or lesser extent. The Church's attitude to women in the early and middle medieval period has been somewhat exaggerated. There was, of course, a strong tradition of misogynist writing following the example of Jerome and others, but there were also many who argued against it.[4] Furthermore, women had always been allowed to teach other women and the very high levels of learning in many convents prior to the fourteenth century is an indication that they did so very well. By the end of the thirteenth and the early fourteenth century Aristotelian concepts were gradually overtaking the Platonic philosophy that had underpinned much religious thinking until then. Aristotle supported the view that women were different in kind from men, that they were males *manqués*. For Plato, on the other hand, men and women were part of the same continuum, at opposite ends perhaps but nevertheless basically joined in their creaturehood before God. Under the influence of Aristotelian ideas of creation and gender, opinions as to the benefit and even the possibility of educating girls hardened and this, in combination with the rise of the universities and their monopolistic claims to knowledge, sent the education of women into a decline from which it was only to emerge several hundred years later.

As lay women, rather than members of established orders, the Beguines were of course in a slightly different position from convent nuns in respect of their freedom to teach. The papal dispensation granted to Beguines to exhort one another to greater faith and good works did much to regularise their activity in the eyes of the Church, at least initially. As we have seen, in the second half of the century there was increasing concern about the tendency of Beguines to discuss theology and to disseminate their ideas. The ideas being disseminated by Beguines included that of the suitability of the priest first promulgated by Pope Gregory VII. In some areas Beguines started to refuse to accept the eucharist from their parish priests, whom they accused of living lives unsuitable for a priest, preferring to do so from a member of one of the mendicant orders. This threat to the power of the Church could not, and did not, go unchallenged. It is clear from the inquisitorial process against Marguerite Porete that the real problem was not so much the ideas themselves as the fact that she was disseminating them in the vernacular to lay people who might be led astray by them.

Different Beguines used different strategies to justify their speaking. Many recount visions in which God gives them explicit instructions to reveal what he had shown them. Mechtild of Magdeburg, for example, writes in Book 2 of her book *Flowing Light of the Godhead*:

> I have been warned about this book
> And this is what I have been told:
> That unless I had it buried
> It would become a prey to fire.
> And so, as had been my wont since childhood,
> Being sad, I began to pray.
> I addressed myself to my beloved
> And said to him: Ah Lord, behold me afflicted
> For the sake of your honour.
> Will you leave me without consolation?
> Then without delay God showed himself to my saddened
>   soul
> Carrying the book in his right hand.
> He said: My beloved, do not despair like that,
> Nobody can burn the truth.
> He who wishes to take this book from my hand
> Must be stronger than I am.
> This book is threefold
> And refers to myself alone.

The parchment that envelops it
Is the image of my humanity, pure, unsullied, just,
That for you suffered death.
The words signify my marvellous Deity:
they flow hour by hour
From my divine mouth into your soul.
The sound of the words proclaims my living Spirit
And expresses with him the just truth.

This is a ringing validation indeed. Any churchman seeking to have the book burned, as they were later to do to Marguerite's book, laid himself open to the accusation of placing Jesus Christ himself on the pyre. There follows a rather two-edged explanation of why such a divine grace should be bestowed on a humble Beguine in preference to some learned churchman:

Whenever I decided to bestow extraordinary gifts
Each time I have sought out the lowest place,
The humblest, the most hidden spot.
The highest mountains cannot assume the burden
Of revealing my graces
For the flood of my Holy Spirit
By its very nature flows towards the valley.[5]

There is here the suggestion that the highest mountains, the priests and churchmen, have insufficient humility to receive such grace. Were they to do so they might perhaps be tempted by the sin of spiritual pride, and assume that they had an active part to play. The Beguine, on the other hand, knows herself to be no more than a channel or receptacle without any personal merit.

Another strategy is that employed by Hadewijch who draws on the Bible for the justification of her speaking. In Poem in Couplets 3 she speaks of Mary Magdalene as the great example to be followed by herself and her audience, and the aspect of Mary Magdalene's life to which she draws attention is the fact of her being the first to have seen the risen Christ. Hadewijch quotes the words of Jesus instructing Mary Magdalene to go and tell what she has seen. This, for Hadewijch, is the justification of her own speaking – she too is obeying the injunction of the risen Christ to tell what she has seen. This justification for speaking is one adopted, explicitly or implicitly, by many women visionaries during the Middle Ages. That Mary Magdalene was a very popular saint among the Beguines can in part be attributed to their affection for the Dominican Order whose patron saint she was, but the significance of the 'Apostle to the Apostles' as a model for these women will have played a part as well.[6] Hadewijch applies Christ's instructions to Mary Magdalene in the garden of Gethsemane directly to herself and to her fellow Beguines, and she does not restrict the command to what she has seen in visions, but applies it more generally to sanction her wider spiritual teaching.

The works of the Beguines reveal a considerable level of theological and spiritual insight. As contemporaries of Thomas Aquinas they were writing before Aristotle's rationalisation of thought had taken hold. If we look for some kind of systematic or speculative rationalisation of theology we will be disappointed. What these women present us with instead is a profound sense of the mystery of God and of his love for humankind. Theology originally means words about God based on experience. The Beguines, like the great monastic theologians before them, speak not with the voice of rational argument, but from the depth of their experience of him as the (W)Holy Other. Faced with the *mysterium tremendum* of God, they attempt to awaken the sense of it in others. The great philosophers of the Islamic and Judaic traditions believed that, in its relation to the divine, human reason has to come to terms with not necessarily the irrational but the a-rational: that which is not against reason but which is different from reason. Prophets and mystics are those who perceive truth, not with their reason, but with their imagination. Their language tends to be full of metaphor, paradox and vivid imagery. The word imagination tends to imply falsehood, fiction. However, in this context it does not mean fiction, it points to a way of understanding the truth which is imagistic, concrete, even sensuous.

Christian imagery for the encounter with God tends to be drawn from two main sources: biblical or church traditions (e.g. Song of Songs), and experience. Tracing the sources of images or groups of images can be very helpful in establishing the currency of certain works or patterns of thought at a given period. Equally, an examination of the frequently small and subtle changes of emphasis in the way an image is used may suggest the significance a particular image or word had for the author. It is precisely in such nuances that distinctive differences between thinkers may be found. One must develop a sensitivity to the ways in which different authors use the image, the ways in which it works within the different texts, for that is where its meaning lies. This is of course a difficult task for readers who are so far removed from the original context of the texts. We can only imagine what the impact of spring might be after a long dark winter with neither electric light nor heating. Nevertheless by analysing the occasions when an image occurs one can gain an insight into some of what the image appears to have meant for the author. The Beguines that form the major part of this study span almost a hundred years between them. Some of the variations in their thought will be due to their particular personalities and insights, others may also be coloured by changing circumstances and the evolution of ideas over time. The concepts discussed should, like the rules mentioned earlier, be read as examples of the range of spirituality current in the milieu of the early Beguines, not in any way as proscriptive. However, they do share certain characteristics, and it is these that I will discuss here. One significant feature is that all these texts were originally written in the vernacular and not in Latin.

These works of Beguine spirituality are among the earliest examples of vernacular literature in the emerging languages of western Europe and are important witnesses to the development of what has become known as 'vernacular theology'. It could be argued that these mystic texts should not be described as theological, and they are indeed far removed from texts of systematic theology, but to the extent that theology is the public utterance of thought about God and the mysteries of the faith, these mystic texts surely qualify despite their different form. The great scholastic and monastic theologians were agreed that their theological methods were ultimately intended to increase the Christian's love for God. These texts, written as they were under the papal dispensation to exhort one another to greater love of God, reflect the same intention. Recent research is making it increasingly clear that we can no longer think of medieval theology just in terms of the two main strands, scholastic and monastic theology, but that we must recognise a third dimension of theology beginning in the thirteenth century – the vernacular theological tradition. The thirteenth century saw the development of new insights into the relationship between God and his creation. The term 'vernacular theology' is a recent coinage to give expression to the recognition that the century also saw the development of new ways of speaking about that relationship.[7]

Religious writing in the vernacular was not simply a case of translation, although there are many examples of this as well, rather it was a new creation revealing a struggle with the boundaries of language and of theology itself. Where texts were translated they were frequently also rewritten in some way.[8] One of the significant aspects of the linguistic context in which theology was articulated in the thirteenth century was the opportunity it gave for challenging the understanding of the roles of men and women. Latin, as the learned second language of the clerical and educational male hierarchy, was not entirely closed to women. However, most women were not given the chance to attain the mastery of Latin required to enable them to take a significant part in matters outside their immediate domestic circle. The use of the vernacular placed women and men on the same footing. In addition, the use of a new language meant that not only the authors but also their audience was new. A different and wider audience was addressed by texts in the vernacular than that addressed by traditional monastic and scholastic theological texts. It is remarkable how the earliest development of theological texts in the vernacular is marked by mystic texts. This is important evidence of the laity's desire for greater spiritual inwardness than their traditional role in the Church had allowed.

Finally, vernacular theology also differed in how it organised and presented its teaching. Scholastic theology is built up using discursive language and rational logic. The great monastic theologians perfected the use of images and metaphors as rumination on biblical texts. As the sermons and treatises of the monastic theologians reveal, similitudes can become a mental habit. They are a way of representing doctrines to the imagination. Vernacular theology in this respect resembles monastic theology in that both make liberal use of imaginative narratives and their teaching uses imaginative logic to make a point. The texts of Beguine spirituality are important witnesses to the growth and development of vernacular theology and one of their key features is that they use what might be called image language in contrast to discursive language. Image language is concerned with exploiting the mind's ability to make affective connections between disparate elements, rather than its capacity for rational logic. It is akin to the traditional storytellers' art of transmitting wisdom through narrative or parable. In the authors' use of imagery, metaphor, paradox and analogy, the meaning is to be found in the interstices of the language, as the mind moves from one element to the next. A major contrast between image and discursive language is that whereas the meaning of a discursive statement tends to be largely static, the impact of an image will be different on a different audience. Even for the same audience/ reader the meaning of any particular image may well change over time as experience, or study, alters their perceptions. Every member of the audience will interpret an image in a slightly different way and the meaning may also be different each time a given person reads or hears it, each time they are, in effect, a different reader. This is most clearly seen in the way poems are read and interpreted. There is no one single interpretation of a poem, rather there is a range of meaning within which numerous interpretations and shades of emphasis are possible.

This is not to take up a deconstructionist position that there is no such thing as a text, or meaning, or the author's intention. Of course, authorial intention is difficult to establish, especially over a gulf such as that which separates us from the Middle Ages, but that is not to say that it did not exist or that it has no relevance for us today. For any serious analysis of theological texts, authorial intention must be a significant element. When dealing with texts written in image language rather than discursive language that authorial intent may be more elusive, but there can be no doubt that it forms one of a range of interpretations suggested by the images used. Which of that range is closest to the intention of the author can only be hazarded after detailed analysis of the texts and comparison with others.

To look at the image language of women mystics without considering the context and the norms which form the background against which they were writing is to risk misinterpreting their message, or at best seeing only a two-dimensional picture. Every period has its own myths, those stories that combine to form the imaginative framework of prejudice according to which behaviour is judged to be acceptable to society or deviant from its norms. Such myths are frequently reflected in the popular literature of the day which tends to act as wish fulfilment rather than as an accurate reflection of what happens in society. Two contemporary examples may serve to illustrate this point. In the 1940s and 1950s myths included that of the perfect wife and loving mother, married to the boy next door who without apparent effort brought home a large salary while she, equally effortlessly, kept the house and their two children immaculate. By the 1970s the myth had changed to that of the wife as superwoman – according to which the wife added holding down a significant and demanding job to her role as perfect wife and loving mother without, however, showing any signs of strain!

Her husband was now more likely to be a high-flying colleague or fellow student than the boy next door, but in its essence the myth had hardly changed. It still presumed marriage, family and the acquisition of material goods as essential elements of success. That these myths have power can be seen in the anger felt by those who consider themselves excluded by them, and that felt by society against those who openly show their lack of regard for the goals set by them.[9] The myths of society, though on the one hand they are intangible and seem even rather trivial, are powerful subconscious influences on society as a whole and on the individual members of it.

In the high Middle Ages, the twelfth, thirteenth and four-teenth centuries, society's myths were also reflected in popular literature: in the literature of courtly love but also in the popular saints' lives of the day. The myth of courtly love, which continued to exert its influence long after the rise of a mer-chant class in the towns, sketched the ideal woman as noble and arrogant. She was desirable but unattainable, demanding and changeable, but ultimately she yielded her power to a man. Men were adventurous heroes, supremely loyal and obedient unto death, and humble even in victory. Another myth was that of the saint, who forsook the world to dedicate themselves to God. In the thirteenth century this myth was augmented by the notion of selfless service to their fellow men and women. Poverty, and spotless purity of life, love for God and dedication to the poor, the sick and the suffering, combined to make a compelling myth and one at least as hard to live up to as that of courtly love.

It should be noted that in the first myth, that of courtly love, the woman plays a largely passive role. It is the man who seeks to win her love by selfless service and carries out her slightest wishes with loyal obedience. The figure of the *amie* in courtly romance is, however, a slightly more active figure. As a recognised part of a couple, she undergoes parallel tests of her loyalty and devotion to establish herself worthy of the knight's love. The second myth, that of the saint, is not so gender specific, although there was a line of thought that held that women were by nature unfit for a spiritual life. In this case the saint was by definition male. Even in those cases where sainthood was seen as potentially accessible to women, society found some ways of embodying the myth more acceptable than others. An example is the reaction experienced by St Clare when she sought to follow St Francis in a life of poverty on the road.[10] The myth of courtly love may have exerted greater influence in secular society than that of the saint, but the power of the myth of the saint should not be underestimated in a period when a number of noble families died out because all their members had embarked on the religious life.

The decision to become a Beguine, rather than to join an established order, will have been influenced by many factors. These factors will have included the lack of opportunities to enter an established order, the high regard in which the lifestyle of the Beguines was held, the desire to live an apostolic life and to serve God within the community, and the greater degree of freedom enjoyed by a Beguine in comparison with an enclosed choir nun. The significance of any particular factor will have changed over the course of time. Most obviously, women who were attracted to becoming Beguines by the high praise the Beguine way of life attracted in the first thirty years of the century would not have been so attracted as the movement began to be criticised rather than praised. Throughout the century, in seeking to follow the new form of religious life, Beguines had willingly and consciously acted to place themselves outside the society which defined the myths. The fact of their having acted, taking their lives into their own hands, placed them outside society's myth of courtly love in which good women do not act. Action was more acceptable in society's myth of the saint, particularly the action of renunciation of the world. The act of rebellion against the world was however the single permissible act before the woman once more placed herself in obedience to men within an order recognised by the Church. The women who became Beguines therefore needed to create new myths of identity to confirm themselves in their choices and to provide a model for their actions.

Different communities create different myths to validate their experience, but all tend to do so by inverting, subverting, an existing myth.[11] In the Beguine communities many took the courtly love myth and inverted it. The work of the Beguines Hadewijch, Mechtild of Magdeburg and Marguerite Porete shows that certain individual Beguines did so, and since they were writing for their communities widely separated in time and place, this suggests that it was a way of thinking that had a certain currency among the Beguine communities in the thirteenth century.

The mysticism of the Beguines is sometimes described as 'bridal' or 'nuptial' mysticism. However, although they do draw on such imagery to a greater or lesser extent, it is not particularly characteristic of their thought. Beguine mysticism has long been acknowledged as a separate category and scholars coined the term *minne-mystiek* (love-mysticism) to describe it. This term, analogous to that for the poetry of courtly love, *minne-lyriek*, points to the most distinctive literary characteristic of the Beguine texts, their close relationship to courtly literature, and reflects the mystics' use of the word *minne* (love) to refer to God. Recently a new term has been suggested which may more clearly indicate the distinctively courtly elements of the Beguines' spirituality, namely *mystique courtoise*.[12] Whichever term is used, it recognises that however marked the element of nuptial imagery may be in these texts, it is not the prime distinguishing feature. More distinctive is the place of trials, persecution and suffering, and the way in which these are presented within the context of *fine amours*, 'courtly love'. That one of the distinguishing features of Beguine spirituality is the way it uses the literary context of *fine amours* is illustrated by a rule surviving from a beguinage in Paris dating from the end of the thirteenth century.[13]

The flowering of the Beguine movement in France was short-lived, as already mentioned, but with the benefit of royal patronage the Parisian beguinages were respected foundations. The rule clearly reflects the courtly ambience in the beguinage, rather than imposing an alien way of thinking on it. It is not especially innovative, similar ideas can be found earlier in the century, but that is its charm in this context. We have a document that comes close to showing us the reality behind the powerful stanzas of, for example, Hadewijch. The fact that the *Regle des fins amans* develops the conceit that the only truly courtly love is that between God and the soul, should not be seen as an argument in favour of a necessarily aristocratic background for the Beguines there or elsewhere. The literature of courtly love will have been equally familiar to the daughters of the rising merchant classes, and the notion that only they were the true *fins amans* will have been equally attractive.

The idea that the highest form of courtly love is the relationship with the divine was not new, nor was it unique to the Beguines. The seeds were sown even within the courtly romance tradition itself with the development of the theme of the holy grail and the pure knight, the pre-eminence of Sir Galahad over Sir Lancelot. Bernard of Clairvaux's sermons on the Song of Songs, drawing on the text as an allegory of the soul's relationship with the heavenly bridegroom, is a prime example of the way the theme was developed in the religious sphere. The relationship between secular and religious courtly literature at this time is not straightforward, nor is the distinction always easy to make. At about this time, a poet in the Low Countries recast a familiar Marian miracle story to emphasise that true courtliness is to be found within the convent, not in the world (here personified as the Virgin Queen of Heaven taking the place of a nun without arousing suspicion).[14] There has been some debate about the intended audience of the *Beatrijs*, whether for an aristocratic or patrician, a secular or religious audience, but the most recent research suggests that it was probably written for a religious audience. The encouragement to think of themselves as truly courtly will have been welcome to both noble and patrician women religious.

The *Regle des fins amans* shows that Beguines too were encouraged to think of themselves as courtly. As we shall see, many of the texts assume the audience's familiarity with the conventions of courtly literature. The authors drew on existing romances to illustrate the points they wished to make about the spiritual life. The distinction between secular courtly and religious literature was far from clear as the Beatrijs romance referred to above illustrates. Another example is that of the Song of Songs. This text was understood to tell the tale of the love of Solomon and the Queen of Sheba, themselves a *figura* (type) for the love between Christ and the Church, God and the soul. The Queen's reaction to Solomon was specifically understood as an example of a soul lost in contemplation of God. It is therefore not surprising to find this quintessentially courtly couple held up as the model for the Beguines. When speaking of four manners of praying, the author describes the fourth manner, contemplation, as 'ravishment' and illustrates it with reference to the Queen of Sheba's reaction to Solomon:[15]

> when the soul is fixed in such meditation (on Jesus Christ and the Trinity), and none of the corporeal senses per-forms its function, it is called ravishment . . . and the Queen of Sheba signifies this to us who heard of Solomon and his riches and came to him from the ends of the earth, and when she found him she said that what she had heard was nothing compared to what she had found. She could not sustain what she saw and fainted. When the soul is in that condition, then she is in contemplation.[16]

That the Beguines are invited to identify with the Queen of Sheba's encounter with Solomon suggests that a mystic encounter with God formed part of their expectations. This form of prayer is entered into by meditation on the glorified humanity of Christ, the divinity joined to human nature, and it is meditation on Christ that leads to meditation on the nature of the Trinity – one God, true man, in three persons, Father, Son and Holy Ghost – the glories of which lead the soul into a state of ravishment. The meditation proposed in the text is not a purely affective dwelling on aspects of the human career of Jesus, it has a more profound intellectual and theological content. In this, as well as in the trinitarian focus for the mystic encounter with God, it resembles the work of other Beguines and is an indication that the level of sophistication found in many Beguine texts was not unique to those few authors whose works have survived, but that it reflects a more general level of culture in beguinages at this time. The author goes on to describe the four ways in which a Beguine should think on Jesus Christ, each assisting in the development of a quality, carefully balancing the need for humility with the need to comfort and encourage: that God became man to acquire humility; his shameful death for us, to acquire patience and comfort in adversity; his resurrection for us, to give hope of glory; that he will judge our actions, to encourage hatred of sin. The mention of the need to acquire patience in adversity may reflect the same general point as other Beguine texts' treatment of suffering, or it could be an indication that the increasingly negative opinion of Beguines was having an effect here as well. Elsewhere in the text the author urges the Beguines to fear not the criticism and calumny of the world, but its praise.[17]

Towards the end of the rule the author includes a short allegory. Similar to that of the *Roman de la Rose*, much of the phraseology is drawn from the *Roman*'s model, the Song of Songs. Conscience wakes in the morning and misses her lover, sighing for his speedy return. Jealousy informs her that the nuns (*li clostries*) have enclosed him and proposes entering their garden to carry him off. Hope then comes to comfort Conscience, and aided by Fine Amours and Charity she is reunited with her love, Jesus Christ, who greets her with the words 'Douce amie, je sui ci'. Then he says to her: 'Turtledove, you have taken me: whosoever is more merciful to me, loves me more.' This allegory illustrates well the blend of religious and secular/courtly language that typifies Beguine spirituality. The relationship between the Beguine and the Godhead is described in courtly terms (*ami/amie*) but the context is that

of the Song of Songs: 'I will rise now, and go about the city in
the streets, and in the broad ways I will seek him whom my
soul loveth: I sought him but I found him not. The watchmen
that go about the city found me: to whom I said, Saw ye him
whom my soul loveth?' (Song of Songs 3:2–3); 'My beloved
spake and said unto me ... O my dove, that art in the clefts
of the rock, in the secret places of the stairs, let me see thy
countenance, let me hear thy voice' (Song of Songs 2:10, 14);
'it is the voice of my beloved that knocketh, saying, Open to
me, my sister, my love, my dove, my undefiled' (Song of Songs
5:2). Interesting from a socio-historical perspective is the
tension between the Beguines and their enclosed sisters
revealed in the allegory. Enclosed themselves, the nuns have
attempted to enclose the divine lover as well. It is the unenclosed Beguines who release him and are greeted by him
with recognition of their status as *fins amans*.

For Marguerite Porete, as for the Paris Beguines, the role of
the soul is that of *amie*, the loyal mistress waiting the return
of her lover. She draws on the familiar romance of Alexander
to illustrate the point. She writes:

> Now in humility listen to a little example of love here
> below and understand how it resembles divine Love. Once
> upon a time there was a lady, a king's daughter, whose
> heart was very worthy and noble and whose spirit was
> noble too, and she lived in a foreign land. Now it happened
> that this lady heard about the great courtliness and
> nobility of King Alexander; at once, in intent, she loved
> him for the great fame of his nobility. But this lady was
> so far from the great lord in whom she had placed her
> love that she could neither see nor possess him. That is
> why she was often disconsolate within, since no other love
> except this sufficed her.
>
> When she saw that this far-off love – though so close
> within her heart – was so far outside her, she thought she
> would seek comfort in her sorrow by somehow imagining
> the appearance of her beloved who so often brought suf-

fering to her heart. Thus she had a portrait painted to the likeness of the king she loved, as close as possible to the way she pictured her beloved to be, according to the sentiment of love that pervaded her. And by means of this image, together with her other practices, she dreamed the king himself.[18]

In case any should miss the point, Marguerite then goes on to explain the allegory in terms of the soul and Christ. Important for the self-perception of the Beguine is the obvious identification of herself with the high-born lady whose spirit was as noble as her birth. Noteworthy is the fact that she loves her lord for the fame of his nobility, not for anything he does for her, and that it is the strength and constancy of her disinterested love that brings him to her. Other Beguines are also scathing about those who love God in order to seek visions and ecstasies.

The courtly context is also central to the work of Hadewijch. She speaks of God as *minne*, love, and since love is a feminine noun this opened the way for her to speak of God as the noble, changeable and unattainable lady of courtly romance. She referred to herself and to those for whom she wrote as the humble lover-knight willing to risk all to satisfy his lady, loyal and obedient till death. There was a tendency to perceive women as being inherently fickle, so this attribution of the female gender to God was a vivid way of representing the many reverses of the mystic life, later to be dubbed 'the dark night of the soul'. It also permitted her and those for whom she was writing to identify with steadfastness, encouraging them to remain steadfast and loyal throughout all the trials they might experience. Finally, the identification of themselves as lover-knights placed upon them the duty to act, to obey the dictates of their lady, which validated their decision to forsake the world and become Beguines and to continue in a life of service to the poor.

There is of course a degree of paradox inherent in the fact of a woman speaking of herself as a man in the same way that

there is when a powerful man such as Bernard of Clairvaux
speaks of himself as a woman as he does in many of his
sermons. Hadewijch was conscious of this and exploited it quite
deliberately in her Poems in Stanzas by occasionally referring
to her female gender in the middle of a passage describing
deeds of knightly valour. In the context of the literature of
courtly love, such a gender shift makes another point. The
desire to be the lady presiding at the court is rooted in the
myth of the society she had left. It reflects a desire to be a
success in the terms of that myth and it is therefore natural
that this desire should be described as an early one. The role of
the fighting knight, humble and constantly having to struggle
again, reflects the reality of service in the life she and her
audience have chosen. By juxtaposing the two images, Hadewijch highlights the difference and confirms her audience in
their choice.

Another feature of Beguine literature, although not unique
to it, is the marked concentration of paradoxes of pain, suffering and love. Women experienced the theological truths of
Christianity, from the virgin birth to the crucifixion, in terms
of paradox, a paradox reflecting their own perceptions of
reality. To be a woman at this time was to be at the centre of a
paradox. We know from the lives of women outside the Church,
mostly of course queens and members of the royal family, that
then as now women loved and were loved, were valued while
they lived and deeply mourned when they died, had influence,
ruled households or kingdoms wisely and well, or badly and
selfishly. However, the models of womanhood held up to their
gaze by the Church did not reflect this reality. Those models
were on the one hand the Virgin Mother – a model ultimately
impossible to emulate – and the virgin martyrs, and on the
other Eve and the inescapably fleshly nature of woman and
her carnality.

The tension between these two models (the one to aspire to,
the other, woman's unavoidable destiny) will not have affected
or influenced the vast majority of women during this period at
all. They will have lived their lives absorbed in the reality of

daily life, uninterested in and unbothered by models or theories of womanhood. But for many women who chose a religious life, the tension will have been inescapable. The models of womanhood available to these women presented woman as wholly carnal (man is to woman as soul is to body), the cause of the Fall (Eve), or a paradox beyond human reach (the Virgin Mother). On the other hand their own experience showed woman less defined by sin and carnality than by a profound love of God. The writings and lives of these women are an absorbing witness to the ways in which they embraced the elements of the paradox and forged from their experience a deeper understanding of their relationship with God.

A further tension for those women aspiring to follow the example of the apostles was the popular dichotomy which presented man as Christ's divinity, and woman as his humanity. It is this tension that is reflected in the paradoxes of suffering and love. Women saw themselves as having a particular privilege when it came to following the example of Christ's suffering love on earth. As we have seen, the thirteenth century was aflame with the desire to live a life of apostolic poverty, following in the footsteps of Christ and his apostles. As the symbol of his humanity, who better qualified to live his life than a woman? That also gave women a special relationship with the suffering they saw around them and the suffering they experienced themselves. The suffering Christ replaced for many of these women the models presented to them by the Church, and pain and suffering patiently borne were the means by which they could follow the example of Jesus. Although they are scathing in their condemnation of exaggerated ascetic practices, the notion that union with Christ is attainable only in suffering is central to the thinking of many of them. For example, Hadewijch writes: 'With the humanity of God you shall live here in suffering and in exile, and with the powerful eternal God you shall love and jubilate inwardly with a sweet confidence and the truth of both these is a single delighting' (Letter 6; Hart, p. 59).[19]

The paradox of suffering in the context of a God they address as Love, has led to some of the most remarkable writing. It has also led to some highly creative use of language as the Beguines sought to express their experience in their vernacular languages, languages not refined by centuries of careful scholastic use. Their use of paradox and homonyms also encourages their audiences to avoid the error of mistaking metaphor and analogy for fact. Hadewijch's use of the word *minne* is a good example of this. The word is rarely capitalised in the manuscripts, and it can be difficult to determine what grammatical role it fulfils in a sentence, so it is hardly surprising that the exact meaning of this central concept of Hadewijch's thought has been the subject of lengthy debate among scholars.[20] Some scholars have taken the view that she uses the word to refer to the Holy Spirit, but there are places where she is clearly speaking of God the Father or the Son. Others have argued that she is speaking not of God, but rather of the personification of his love for humankind, or possibly of the soul's love for God. These explanations too can be countered by examples where she is definitely speaking of God. Hadewijch's choice of *Minne* (Love) as the name for God enables her to exploit the ambiguity inherent in the word to good effect. Indeed, it is the multivalence of the term that gives it its strength. The ambiguity inherent in the use of the word *minne* helps to illustrate a profound point, namely that the love wherewith we love God is the love wherewith he first loved us, and is indeed the love that is God.[21] Since the word is only rarely capitalised in the original manuscripts, it can be very difficult to determine when it is being used as a proper noun referring to God, and when as a noun referring to the emotion, whether God's love for humankind or the soul's love for God. This difficulty mirrors that of the original audience of these texts who will have listened to them, rather than read them as we do now. A striking example occurs at the end of Poem in Couplets 15:

> O love, were I love
> And with love to love you, love,

O love, for love grant that love
May know love wholly as love.

(Poem in Couplets 15:49–52)

Her use of the word *minne* to refer to the Divine also enables her to say things about her experience of God which might otherwise be hard to understand. She is able to speak of the pain she experiences in her relationship with God in sufficiently ambiguous language to make it acceptable. One example is in Poem in Couplets 16 where she describes the seven names of God, of which the seventh is 'Hell'. She writes:

Forever to be in unrest,
Forever assault and new persecutions,
To be wholly devoured and wholly engulfed
In her (Love's) unfathomable nature,
To founder in incandescence and in cold every hour
In the deep high darkness of Love
This exceeds the pains of hell.
He who knows Love and her comings and goings
Has experienced and can understand
Why it is truly appropriate
That Hell should be the highest name of Love.

(Poem in Couplets 16:158–164)

Hadewijch may here be speaking of her experience of loving God rather than of her experience of God, although the distinction is meaningless to the extent that these two are the same.

Such use of the word *minne* for the divine is not unique to Hadewijch. Beatrijs of Nazareth describes her experience in similar terms:

Love leaves her [the blessed soul] neither peace, nor respite, nor rest. Love raises her up and casts her down, suddenly draws her close only to torment her later, makes her die to bring her back to life again, wounds her and heals her, drives her to madness and then makes her wise again. It is in this way that love draws her to a higher state [of being].[22]

The ambiguity created by the Beguines' use of *minne* is one way for them to speak of their perception that, in the relationship between creature and creator, there are elements of horror and awe, the wrath of God, as well as fascination and love.[23] The Beguines are acutely aware of God as 'other', of the *mysterium tremendum* of God. Aspects of this are of course perceptible throughout their work, and in all the images they employ. However, it is particularly closely linked to their understanding of the role of suffering. The fear and awe evoked by the realisation of the immensity of the gulf that exists between God and his creatures is, for the Beguines, the other side of the intimacy they experience sharing with him the bed of their pain. A powerful sense of God as the supremely 'other' permeates all of Hadewijch's work. She is not afraid to face the potential horror of the gulf that separates God from his creatures, nor does she shy away from the *tremendum* aspect of God, from the awe-fullness of the Divinity. In her vision of the Trinity in Vision 1 she turns to find herself on the edge of an abyss filled with a terrifying whirlpool which represents Divine fruition:

> I turned around and I saw standing before me a cross like crystal, clearer and whiter than crystal. And through it a great space was visible. And in front of the cross I saw a seat like a disc, more radiant that the sun in its most radiant power and beneath the disc stood three columns . . . And in the middle under the disc, a whirlpool revolved in such a frightful manner and was so terrible to see that heaven and earth would be astonished and made fearful by it. The seat that resembled a disk was eternity. The three pillars were the three names by which the wretched ones who are far from Love understand him. The pillar like fire is the name of the Holy Ghost. The pillar like topaz is the name of the Father. The pillar like amethyst is the name of the Son. The profound whirlpool, which is so frightfully dark, is divine fruition in its hidden storms. In this mighty place sat the one whom I was

seeking and with whom I desired to be one in fruition.
(Vision 1:216–247; Hart, p. 267)

Noteworthy in this passage is the suggestion that the one
Hadewijch seeks is the unity of the one God. The three
elements of the Trinity support the One and are the names or
aspects by which the One is known by those who are far off.[24]
The definition of *minne* as the essential unity of the Supreme
Being is particularly interesting in view of the debate that
there has been about the exact import of the term for
Hadewijch.

In addition to ambiguity, the Beguines also make use of
paradox to illustrate the unfathomable nature and fascination
of God. A good example is Hadewijch's Poem in Couplets 13.
This is little more than a list of paradoxes which gradually
overwhelm the listener in much the same way as the verse
from Poem in Couplets 15 quoted above does. For example:

That which is sweetest of love is her storms;
Her deepest abyss is her most glorious form;
To go astray in her, that is to come near;
To starve for her sake, that is to feed and to taste;
Her despair is to be in bliss;

(Poem in Couplets 13:1–5)

In this way Hadewijch, like the other Beguines, uses language
and images to show that all speech about God must be metaphorical – words when applied to God do not mean the same
as when applied to creatures.[25] The ways in which Hadewijch
deliberately moves between the meanings of *minne* and other
ambiguous terms alerts her audience to the error of mistaking
metaphor and analogy for fact. For Hadewijch and the other
Beguines the *mysterium tremendum* aspect of the Deity is
central to their understanding of him. Their sense of horror
and awe, as well as the fascination and the love, is the product
of the acknowledgement of their creaturehood before God.
They articulate what many have felt, namely the wonder at
the love that is God while trembling in fear and awe at the

gulf that separates Creator from creature. The images they use to express their sense of the awfulness of God include those of the whirlpool and the abyss, and, like their use of *minne*, these images speak also of the immensity of the love and the extraordinary grace of union. For Hadewijch, for example, the abyss is peculiarly the place of closest encounter with God. The Beguines' language and imagery illustrates their embrace of the paradox of pain and suffering as part of their experience of a God that is Love. It enables them to accept the *tremendum* aspect of God, the horror as well as the love, indeed the horror of the love. This aspect of Beguine spirituality is foreign to much contemporary Christianity, which emphasises rather the accessibility of God, and that may be where its value lies for us today.

3. FOUR LIVES: FOUR TEXTS

The most important vernacular mystic texts of the thirteenth
century are the work of four women: Mechtild of Magdeburg,
Beatrijs of Nazareth, Hadewijch, and Marguerite Porete. The
quality of their writing suggests that they were not writing in
isolation, that they were not the only articulate, literate
women in their circles. Indeed the uncertainty that continues
over the authorship of some of the texts in the manuscripts of
Hadewijch's work is an indication of the high quality of writing
we have come to expect in Beguine circles in the Low Countries
at that time.[1] However, although much Beguine writing has
certainly been lost, it would be wrong to see all beguinages as
the medieval equivalent of the women's colleges of Oxford and
Cambridge. The vast majority of Beguines were not unusually
creative or high-powered theological thinkers, but simply pious
women seeking to do what they could to improve the lot of
some of those they saw around them, and by so doing to atone
in some measure for the role their families had and continued
to have in oppressing the poor.

BEATRIJS OF NAZARETH

The life of Beatrijs of Nazareth, which we know from her
vita and from that of her father, the blessed Bartholomeus,
illustrates a number of the features of the religious feeling of
the thirteenth century discussed in a previous chapter. She
was born in 1200, the youngest daughter of a wealthy and
highly respected burger couple in the town of Tienen, in the
vicinity of Leuven. After the death of his wife in 1207, Beatrijs'

father responded to the religious enthusiasm of the day by founding three Cistercian convents: Bloomendael (1210), Maagdendael (1221) and Nazareth (1236). In 1215, he, his three daughters and one son became Cistercians while the other son had already entered the Premonstratensian Order in 1207. Beatrijs enjoyed an excellent education, even before her entry into the convent, at a Beguine school in Zoutleeuw. Her *vita* describes her as unusually gifted, being able to recite all 150 Psalms by heart at five years of age. She learnt Latin and was able to read Augustine's *De Trinitate* as well as works by such twelfth-century theologians as Richard and Hugh of St Victor. Even allowing for a degree of hagiographical exaggeration, this helps to confirm the high standard of education available in Beguine schools in the early years of the century and, by extension, the high standard of education enjoyed by those women who became Beguines and taught in them.

After one year at Bloomendael, Beatrijs went to the convent at Rameia to learn the art of copying and illumination. The one year she spent there was to prove very important for her spiritual formation as she met and formed a lasting friendship with the nun Ida of Nivelles. Ida was only slightly older than Beatrijs but already enjoyed a rich spiritual life of ecstasy and visions. She acted as Beatrijs' guide and example, and although they were parted after only a year they frequently had visions about each other thereafter. After the foundation of Maagdendael, Beatrijs and her sister moved there before moving once again to their father's final foundation, the convent at Nazareth in 1236. In 1237 Beatrijs was elected prioress, which she remained until her death in 1268, only a few years after her father.[2]

A key visionary experience in Beatrijs' spiritual development occurred while she was at Rameia. The liturgy caused her to fall into a meditation during which she was lifted up and saw with her inner, spiritual, not fleshly, eyes the holy Trinity surrounded by the heavenly host. It is significant that the vision was of long duration, was prompted by the liturgy, and did not reveal anything new, rather it gave form and made

perceptible what was already known. She had a similar experience in Maagdendael in 1231, once again prompted by the
liturgy, during which she learned that her place in heaven was
assured. According to the author of her *vita* she continued to
enjoy visions while in Nazareth. However, I agree with Kurt
Ruh that the very different character of these visions suggests
that they may have been inserted by the author of the *vita*.
Ruh argues that he may have felt the need to include these
visions in order to present the final stages of Beatrijs' life as
status perfectionem.[3]

The only work we have by Beatrijs of Nazareth is a short
prose text in Middle Dutch, *De seuen mannieren van minne*,
'The Seven Manners (or Ways) of Loving', which exists in just
three manuscripts. There is in addition a version in the Latin
vita, but this has been much altered. The effect of these alterations has been to cast doubt on the authenticity of the Dutch
text, which is unfortunate since the Dutch text itself is a
perfectly coherent whole. No compelling arguments have been
put forward for preferring the version in the *vita*, and it may
be no more than an in-built preference for an 'authorised'
version. I am therefore inclined to agree with Ruh that there
is no substantive reason to doubt the authenticity of the
Dutch.[4] The author of the *vita* based his work on Beatrijs'
extensive spiritual diaries, although he admits to altering or
omitting sections when in his view they were more likely to
do harm than good. This too argues strongly in favour of the
Middle Dutch text's authenticity against that of the Latin –
there is no reason to suppose the priest limited his editorial
efforts to the diaries alone. Unfortunately Beatrijs' spiritual
diaries have not survived – they would have been the earliest
autobiographical document in Dutch. It has been suggested
that they may have been destroyed by the author of the *vita*
when he had completed his work, and it does seem likely that
clerical distrust of vernacular discussions of theology may have
prompted the diaries' destruction as well as the scribal alterations. However, despite the efforts of the author to mould

the diaries into a traditional hagiographical *vita* with the tri-partite structure of *status inchoantium* (initiation), *status proficientium* (proficiency), *status perfectionem* (perfection), Beatrijs' personal voice is still perceptible in some of the more didactic sections.

The *seuen mannieren van minne* is the product of Beatrijs' long reflection on the powerful nature of her experience of God. The *seuen mannieren* are not presented as steps in an ascending order, rather they are presented as different ways of experiencing *minne* in the course of a life dedicated to the love of God. Although the *vita* describes in detail Beatrijs' ascetic life, she makes little mention of the need for asceticism in this text.

The Seven Manners of Loving

The first manner is that of desire, and desire must rule the heart for as long as it takes to remove all resistance and to restore the soul to its condition as made in the image of God. The effort to restore the likeness will take a lifetime of dedicated effort. The soul should be careful to avoid everything that would get in the way.

> This manner of loving is of such great purity and nobility that it surely comes from love and not from fear, because fear causes [one] to work and to be virtuous, to do and to leave undone, for fear of the anger of the Lord and the judgement of that just judge or his eternal vengeance or temporal punishments. But love works towards and is fixed on only purity and majesty and highest nobility, as she is herself and in her own being.[5]

The second manner of loving is that of service, service without measure. She writes:

> And like a lady serves her lord because of her great love and without any reward – and it pleases her that she may serve him, and that he permits her to serve him – in this

way she desires to serve love with love without measure,
beyond measure, and beyond human sense or reason with
all the service of faithfulness.[6]

The evidence that a soul is in this condition is its cheerfulness
and alacrity to serve others, grateful to have found things to
do to serve love. The concept of unconditional service is found,
among others, in the work of Bernard of Clairvaux and Richard
of St Victor, and it is also an important one for Hadewijch.

The third manner concentrates on the soul's longing to
satisfy love. This longing can never be satisfied, and the con-
stant unsatisfied striving causes storms of insatiable desire in
the soul, and agonies similar to the pains of hell.

And a source of great pain is that she must desire what
she may not obtain . . . and it is to her as though living she
dies, and dying feels the pains of hell. And her whole life
is hellish, cruel, and painful because of the dreadfulness
of the fearful desire which she can never satisfy, nor pacify,
nor fulfil. She must stay in this suffering until our lord
comforts her and places her in a different manner of loving
and of desire and in even closer knowledge of him.[7]

This description of the storms of love and the pain suffered by
the loving soul is very like Hadewijch's experience. Similarly,
the idea that the suffering is caused by *minne* herself is not
infrequent in Beguine spirituality.

The fourth manner speaks of the great delights experienced
by the soul. *Minne* is described as overwhelming the soul in
intensity – the soul experiences the closeness of God in
freedom, sweetness and clarity. Absorbed in the abyss of love
the soul becomes love. 'And then she feels that all her senses
are sanctified in love and that her will has become love and
that she has sunk so deeply into the abyss of love, and been
swallowed up by it, and is herself become love.'[8] Like the other
Beguines, Beatrijs is untroubled by the later concern to make
a clear difference between a *unitas spiritus*, in which distinction is maintained, and the union without distinction of the

mystic with God.[9] Her experience of union with God took her beyond the orthodox conception of union. She ends the description of the fourth manner of loving with a description of the soul in this condition as a vessel that is so full that if it is moved it cannot help overflowing.

The fifth manner describes the other side of the coin of *minne*. While in the fourth manner the soul experiences the overwhelming sweetness of love, here she shows her strength. The imagery used is not unlike that of the third manner of the storms of love, but whereas in the third manner Beatrijs describes the pain of endless striving to satisfy love, here it is the experience of love itself that causes her to feel that her arteries burst, her blood boils, the very marrow in her bones is consumed. She writes: 'If she is in this [state], then she is so powerful in spirit, so enterprising in her heart and strong in body and so swift in works and busy without and within that she feels that everything about her is active and employed even if she appears to be at rest.'[10] Beatrijs also develops an extended metaphor of the wounds of love which counterbalances the beautiful descriptions of the sweetness of love in the previous section.

The sixth manner, for the first time, refers to it being more advanced than those previously described. She speaks of the soul as having progressed and calls it the Bride of the Lord. Beatrijs describes how the soul now suffers all things gladly, and practises love easily. To illustrate the point that the soul is now perfectly ruled by *minne*, Beatrijs uses an image much used by Mechtild of Magdeburg, that of the *husurouwe* who rules her household well and does as she pleases.

> Then love makes her so bold and so free that she fears neither people nor the devil, nor angels, nor saints, nor God himself in all that she does or leaves undone, in work or in rest. And she feels clearly that love is working within her as much when the body is at rest as when it is working. She knows well and feels that love is not in work nor in pain in those whom she rules.[11]

The soul is now the *imago dei* restored and this is closely parallel to the condition later described by Marguerite Porete. But, adds Beatrijs as a caution, all who wish to reach this manner of loving must first endure the pain and struggle of previous stages.

Although the sixth manner ends suggesting that all that follows it is the beatific vision in heaven, the seventh manner describes the soul's continued longing. 'She cannot forget her misery/exile, her desire cannot be fulfilled, her longing causes her to suffer piteously, and this tortures and torments her beyond measure and without pity.'[12] The soul can find no rest, but is always painfully aware of the distance which separates her from God even at the moment of greatest closeness. 'For love does not let her rest nor have repose nor be at peace. Love pulls her up and holds her down . . . she gives death and delivers life, she heals and then wounds again . . . Thus she pulls her to a higher state of being.'[13] The fickle behaviour of *minne* is the way the soul mounts higher towards her goal of union with God in heaven. 'There the soul is united with her bridegroom and becomes one spirit with him in indivisible faithfulness and eternal love.'[14]

From this brief synopsis it is clear that Beatrijs shares many of the same themes that dominate the work of her contemporary Hadewijch.[15] Especially important for an understanding of the particular nature of Beguine spirituality are the themes of service, the inability to satisfy God, the everburning longing for God in storms of love, loving without measure, and the paradox of love as pain and delight. These themes also reveal the debt owed by these women to the work of the Cistercians and Victorines of the previous century.

MECHTILD OF MAGDEBURG

Mechtild was born in the vicinity of Magdeburg in 1207, probably of wealthy and possibly aristocratic parents. In 1230, at twenty-three years of age, she moved to Magdeburg to take up her life as a Beguine. We know from a comment in her book that Mechtild chose to go to Magdeburg because she knew almost no one in that town. However, it is probably not a coincidence that Magdeburg is also where St Norbert, the founder of the Premonstratensian Order, spent the last years of his life as archbishop and is buried. In 1206, just before Mechtild's birth, a fire swept through Magdeburg, destroying most of the town including the churches. One of the few buildings to survive was Norbert's stone-built monastery. As the Beguines appear to have been a development from the lay sisters of the Premonstratensian and Cistercian Orders, it seems likely that there will have been some kind of community of devout lay women in Magdeburg for some time. When Mechtild arrived in Magdeburg two great new Gothic churches were being built in stone, and she will have seen them completed.[16] After forty years in Magdeburg (during which she will have experienced first hand the shift in public opinion from general admiration to suspicion), she joined the convent in Helfta in 1270, dying there around 1282. The community in Helfta followed the Benedictine rule but was very much influenced by Cistercian spirituality.[17] There she joined a remarkable group of women – Gertrude the Great of Helfta (1256–1302), Mechtild of Hackeborn (1241–1299), and her elder sister Abbess Gertrude of Hackeborn (1232–1292) – all of them gifted mystics and visionaries in their own right.

Mechtild's book *Fliessende Licht der Gottheit* (Flowing Light of the Godhead) consists of seven books and was written in her native low-German dialect.[18] However, the original has not survived and the text has been preserved in a high-German version created in the circle of Heinrich von Nordlingen in Basel between 1343 and 1345, and a Latin translation of books I–VI made in the Dominican house at Halle not long after Mechtild's death. This Latin version is important for an understanding of the way the text developed as it was made of a copy of books I–VI made before 1270. Mechtild's book is divided into seven books. Books I–V were written between 1250 and 1259, book VI between 1260 and 1270, book VII between 1271 and 1282 in Helfta. The first five books were written with the encouragement and assistance of Mechtild's Dominican confessor, Heinrich of Halle, while she was still in Magdeburg and it has been suggested that books I–IV were in fact conceived as a whole by Mechtild herself.[19] The sixth book has a somewhat different perspective from the first books, but is nevertheless complementary to them. The seventh book, written in Helfta, is distinct from the earlier books and does not appear to have been edited. It may therefore be closest to Mechtild's own words.

Despite the time-scale of the creation of the work, and the very different contexts in which the different sections were written, many commentaries assume that what is true for one section must also be true for another. The ordering of the visions into a sequence of books was the work of her editor and spiritual advisor, Heinrich von Halle, so the temptation to read the text as if the visions occurred in that chronological order should be resisted. Most of the visions that draw heavily on nuptial imagery occur early on in the book, leaving until later those that have more domestic imagery. This corresponds to what God says about Mechtild in one of her later visions: 'Your childhood was the playmate of my Holy Spirit, your youth the bride of my Humanity, and now your old age is the mistress of the house of my Divinity' (Book 7:3), so the ordering may reflect the original chronology, but we cannot be sure.

The book affords the modern reader a glimpse of some aspects of the life of a Beguine, and it reflects an acute awareness of the spiritual dangers surrounding Beguines in the world. Mechtild quotes her confessor on more than one occasion and, as we have seen, responds to possible criticism of her book by recourse to dialogues with God in which God reiterates his command that she write her experiences down. However contrived some of her visions seem, they nevertheless give evidence of a very real fear of the accusation of heresy which must have been a feature of most Beguines' lives as the century wore on.

The *Fliessende Licht der Gottheit* has often been described as bridal mysticism and much of Mechtild's imagery is reminiscent of the Song of Songs, but the essence of her spirituality is more complicated than that label suggests. Even where her imagery is clearly nuptial, her treatment of it is rather different from that of, for example, Bernard of Clairvaux. There is a greater warmth and familiarity in the relationship between the soul (Mechtild) and God. In the earlier books she attributes to God a passionate longing for the soul similar to that felt by the soul for God,[20] and in the later ones she portrays a relationship of easy intercourse reminiscent of a long-established marriage. For Mechtild, as for the other Beguines, love is knowledge. *Amor ipse intellectus est*, William of St Thierry's phrase describing the point at which human love and intellect are transformed within the soul in conformity with the divine, expresses Mechtild's conception of *minne* as she experienced it.

Like Hadewijch and Beatrijs, Mechtild also speaks of the violent attacks of *minne*. In this, her work is also reminiscent of Richard of St Victor's *De quatuor gradibus violentae caritatis* (Of four grades of violent love), although for Mechtild the stages are successive experiences while Richard speaks of them as increasing grades of severity. Like Hadewijch, Mechtild's most profound understanding of *minne* is of the merciless withdrawal of her presence. The theme of *amor deficiens* will also have been familiar to the Beguines from the work of Richard of St Victor and William of St Thierry. This withdrawal is not a passing phase, a time of trial to establish the mystic's worthiness, rather it is the highest manifestation of the awful presence of God, and Mechtild goes so far as to search out the absence of God, asking him to withdraw from her and to allow her to sink lower.[21] It is there, in the depths of despair when the soul feels furthest away from God, that Mechtild experiences the comfort and presence of *minne*. Like the other Beguines, she can truly be said to sink deep into the heights of the sweetness of *minne*.

HADEWIJCH

Hadewijch is the third thirteenth-century mystic Beguine, and possibly the greatest of the three, but we know even less of her life than we do of the other two. Her work, found in five closely related manuscripts, comprises forty-five poems in stanzas, thirty-one letters, fourteen visions, a list of 'perfect ones', and a collection of some twenty-nine other poems of which sixteen are thought certainly to be by her. The authenticity of the remaining thirteen poems and a further prose text known as the *Twee-vormich Tractaetken*, the 'Two-fold Tract', which do not occur in all the manuscripts has been in doubt since the manuscripts were discovered in the last quarter of the nineteenth century. Doubts have also been raised about the authenticity of Letter 28.[22] From internal evidence, principally from the list of the 'perfect ones', it seems likely that she was writing in the first half of the century.[23] On the fly-leaf of one of the manuscripts, in a sixteenth-century hand, are the words 'Hadewijch de Antverpia' by which she has become known, but so far no evidence linking her to this city or to any other has been found. The five manuscripts containing her work are very closely related and all originated in and around Brussels. It would seem possible therefore that she may have had links with that city herself, although no evidence for this has yet been found.

Her work shows a very high degree of learning. Her poetic skill and understanding of the conventions of the poetry of courtly love is considerable. She clearly read Latin and knew the work of William of St Thierry, the Victorines, Bernard of Clairvaux, and other theologians.[24] This fits in well with her likely date early in the century and with the fact that many of the early Beguines came from wealthy or aristocratic families. However, a problem has always been that no trace of her has been found in any of the archives relating to possible families. Ruh has recently suggested that this could be because the family disowned her for having disgraced the family name by becoming a Beguine in preference to joining a recognised

Order.[25] Although possible, the high reputation Beguines enjoyed in the early part of the century makes the explanation seem rather forced. The suggestion elsewhere that the information was supressed in order to protect Hadewijch is perhaps more likely at a time when marriage by kidnap and rape was not uncommon.[26] Equally possible is that she was a daughter of one of the many families which died out at that time when the parents and their offspring entered different forms of the religious life. There could however be an alternative explanation for her considerable knowledge of the poetics of trouvere poetry. It is possible that Hadewijch, like Alheid who left her noble mistress in Nuremburg in 1211 to live a life of penance and was later invited to lead a group of like-minded women, may herself have been a troubadour or harpist.[27]

It is Hadewijch's poetry that has received the most attention. The forty-five Poems in Stanzas are written in the form and using the conventions of the courtly love lyric – the faithful lover-knight bemoans his lot in serving a fickle and demanding lady. Linguistically this is quite an achievement because the Dutch language does not behave at all like French and has rigid rules for word-order, so the complex rhyme schemes are no mean feat. The poems rank among the best in Dutch of any period. What makes them even more interesting, however, is that Hadewijch uses the form to illustrate her relationship to God, describing herself as the faithful knight, and God, to whom she like the other Beguines refers as *minne*, as the fickle demanding lady. This works well linguistically as the Dutch noun *minne* is feminine and consequently takes feminine adjectives and pronouns.[28] Hadewijch does not confine her use of the word *minne* for God to her Poems in Stanzas – it permeates her work.

The theology of her texts is extremely interesting. Like the other Beguines, she puts forward a hard doctrine of suffering and being rejected by people on earth as the only place where union is possible. Suffering is not the means to obtain favour, nor is it primarily a way of paying for sin, rather she sees that the creature can resemble God only in human suffering. Woman, symbolising the flesh of Christ's humanity, was uniquely privileged to follow his example in suffering here on earth. And by this emulation to approach Christ, to become comparable with him, and hence to become one. It bears repeating that, for Hadewijch as for the other Beguines, suffering was not seen simply as a way of expiating sin, or as a way of earning or deserving union in some way. Nor does Hadewijch speak of obtaining union in the midst of suffering or by means of suffering. For Hadewijch suffering *is* union. The need to suffer with Christ's humanity is first expounded to Hadewijch by Christ in her visions:

> Furthermore, he said, I give you a new commandment: If you wish to be like me in my humanity as you desire to possess me wholly in my divinity, so you shall desire to be poor, miserable, and despised by all. And all troubles will taste sweeter to you than all earthly pleasures; do not in any way let them sadden you, for they will be beyond human nature to bear. If you wish to follow love . . . you shall become as an alien among people, and you will be so despised and so unhappy that you will not know where to lodge for a single night, and all persons will fall away from you and forsake you, and no one will be willing to wander about with you in your distress and your weakness. (Vision 1; Hart, p. 268.)

This commandment demands much, so it is not surprising that in Letter 6 she writes: 'We all wish to be God with God, but God knows there are few of us who want to live as man with God's humanity' (Letter 6; Hart, p. 61). Many of her poems speak of the psychological pain and confusion involved in obeying the commandment. For example, she writes:

> Love then causes more sorrows
> than there are stars in heaven.
> The number of these sorrows must be unspoken,
> the great weighty burdens remain unweighed

> There is nothing which can compare with it,
> so it is best not to attempt the comparison.
> Although the part I have borne is small
> I shudder that I live.
> How life can cause him to shudder and to suffer
> who has risked his all for all
> and is driven far off to wander in the dark
> whence he fears never to return
> and is crushed in a storm of despair;
> what suffering can be compared to that pain?
>
> (Poem in Stanzas 17:17–30)

Nevertheless, the message of Hadewijch's mystic theology is that it is at the moment of feeling lost in the dark, of feeling crushed by despair, that (wo)man comes closest to being one with the God-Man. Hadewijch learns that it is only in the suffering caused by the absence of love that desire becomes so great as to become one with that love. In Letter 8 she speaks of the doubt and distrust engendered by love's withdrawal as 'unfaith'. This condition to which the soul is driven by the torments of *minne* is the point where she no longer believes in the faithfulness of *minne*.[29]

> This unfaith is higher than any fidelity that is not of the abyss. I mean than a fidelity that allows itself to rest peacefully without the full possession of love, or than a fidelity that takes pleasure in what it has in the hand. This noble unfaith has a greatly enlarged consciousness . . . this unfaith can neither feel nor trust love, so much does unfaith enlarge desire. And unfaith never allows desire any rest in any fidelity but, in the fear of not being loved enough, continually distrusts desire.
>
> (Letter 8; Hart, p. 65.)

It is unfaith, born of suffering, that drives desire to become ever greater until it becomes as great as love itself. In her thirteenth vision she is shown the eight gifts of love of which the eighth and highest is 'unfaith'. Indifferent to the consolations of *minne*, the soul takes her on on her own terms. The frustrated desire of unfaith is what enlarges the soul to the point that it can become one with God. She writes:

> Unfaith made them so deep that they wholly engulfed *minne* and dared to fight her with sweet and bitter. What love gives is soured, consumed, and swallowed up; what she takes that becomes riches by the great strength of the experience of the demand of love [to be] every hour as great as herself. (Vision 13; Hart, p. 300.)

The central paradox of Hadewijch's spirituality is that to suffer with God's humanity and to rejoice with his divinity is, to use her own words, 'a single rejoicing' (Letter 6; Hart, p. 65). The ultimate mystic experience is for her the recognition that God is most intimately present at the moment when he seems most absent. Spiritual union with God consists not in ecstasies, visions and supernatural sweetness, which Hadewijch, like the other Beguines, dismisses as juvenile, but in serving one's fellow (wo)man while being painfully rejected and despised. In this way, Hadewijch, like the other Beguines, developed a spirituality which does not need the silence of contemplation but is practised in the course of daily life. She acknowledges the reality of the doubts and uncertainties about God felt by many. The doubts and uncertainties she encountered herself, her sense of the absence of God and the desire for his presence, caused her real psychological suffering. She learned that it is within the sense of God's absence that union takes place – that ultimately the only possible point of contact between the creature and God is in the suffering, loving, humanity of Christ's final question on the cross: 'My God, my God, why hast thou forsaken me?' Her definition of union as being possible only within suffering offers a way of making sense of the pain and suffering of life on earth, turning that suffering into triumph. She describes the union achieved within suffering in various ways. Following her twelfth-century exemplars, she speaks of it as a condition in which both the soul and God remain for ever distinct. However, she also describes it in terms which foreshadow the fourteenth-century mystics: of becoming one with *minne*, of being one with God.[30] Speaking from her own experience like the other Beguines, and untroubled by later concerns about heresy, she saw no difficulty in using both types of description. In Poem in Couplets 12 she writes of union:

> And that kiss will be with one single mouth,
> And to fathom the one single ground,
> And with a single gaze to understand all
> That is, and was, and shall be.
>
> (Poem in Couplets 12:87–90)

Mechtild of Magdeburg writes in similar terms:

> So, Lord, your blood and mine are one, untainted;
> Your voice and mine are one, undivided;
> Your robe and mine are one, immaculate;
> Your mouth and mine are one, unkissed.
>
> (Book 2:25)

Such powerful language of complete union with God is strongly reminiscent of Eckhart, yet further indication of the extent to which his spirituality was influenced by the Beguines who came before him.

In discussions of Beguine literature one will occasionally come across references to Hadewijch II. This term is increasingly being used to refer to one or both parts of a collection of poems that occurs in some but not all of the manuscripts of Hadewijch's work. I have argued that the first part of the collection, Mengeldichten 17–24 in Van Mierlo's edition, are contemporary with Hadewijch.[31] They share many of the literary features of her imagery and poetics, and moreover the paradox of union with God through suffering on earth with his humanity, union as *vercrighen in ontbliuen* ('obtaining within lack'), is central to the mystic theology of these poems as it is to that of Hadewijch. The second part of the collection, Mengeldichten 25–29, appears to me to be of slightly later date and by several different authors.[32] (Mengeldichten 1–16 occur in all the main Hadewijch manuscripts and have been translated by Hart as 'Poems in Couplets'.) In 1923 Bouman drew attention to the marked similarities between some of the Mengeldichten and texts attributed to Eckhart.[33] At the time, the assumption was that the influence could only have been from Eckhart to the authors of the texts in question, not the other way round. The similarities were therefore interpreted as evidence that the poems were written in the fourteenth, rather than the thirteenth, century. Recent scholarship has shown that Eckhart was influenced by the mystic women who came before him, so that similarity is not of itself sufficient to suggest the likely date of authorship. It is time for a reassessment of the views which saw the Mengeldichten as later than the rest of the work in the Hadewijch manuscripts and therefore as inferior. These views depended on the now fortunately increasingly dated concentration on the creative individual, implying standards of judgement which are hardly appropriate in the case of medieval texts. They also reinforced the tendency to look for a canon within the canon rather than seeking a hermeneutic for each and every text which has become part of the canonical literature by virtue of its inclusion in the manuscripts. Whether or not some or all of these poems are by Hadewijch, they are further evidence of a lively tradition of spiritual writing in the vernacular in the beguinages of the Low Countries during the thirteenth century. Another poem, found in a manuscript of 1351, must also have originated in the same circles as it is closely related to one of Hadewijch's poems.[34] Some of the manuscripts of Hadewijch's work contain a further short prose text known as the *Twee-vormich Tractaetken*.

MARGUERITE PORETE

Not very much more is known of the life of Marguerite Porete than we know of that of Hadewijch, although we know rather more about her death. Marguerite was burnt at the stake as a lapsed heretic in Paris on 1 June 1310. The inquisitorial process suggests that she was a Beguine from Hennegau or Valenciennes. A beguinage had been established in Valenciennes in 1239 by the Bishop of Cambrai, and she may well have lived there. Marguerite's lack of respect for the hierarchy of the established Church certainly points to her having been a Beguine. In many ways she epitomises all that Mechtild of Magdeburg was afraid of and cautioned against so strongly – contempt for the established Church and the setting up of her own opinions in opposition to the advice of her spiritual guide. Indeed, Marguerite dismisses rather contemptuously the notion that she, or those who follow her, might need any spiritual guidance from priests in the established Church. What makes the case of Marguerite particularly interesting for the history of vernacular theology is that, although the Inquisition did find heretical statements in her book *Le Mirouer des Simples Ames* (The Mirror of Simple Souls), what caused her to be condemned to death was not the writing of the book, rather its dissemination. The book had been condemned in 1306 and was publicly burned in Valenciennes. It was only when she continued to disseminate the work that she herself was finally condemned in Paris. Matters so weighty and so likely to confuse the unlearned into heretical opinions should not be widely available in the vernacular. In the light of his own posthumous condemnation for heresy, it is interesting to note the extent to which Eckhart was influenced by her work, and phrases reminiscent of many of his statements can be found in the *Mirouer*. Although in the decades immediately following her condemnation the book continued to be held suspect, within a hundred years of her death it was being widely circulated throughout Europe in Latin and in numerous translations as the work of an anonymous Carthusian monk. Ascribed to an anonymous male member of an Order known for its severity and conservatism the book was acceptable, even admired; written by a lay woman it was deeply suspect.

The central theme of the *Mirouer* is the annihilation of the soul by the abolition of personal will. The soul no longer wills anything of itself, only the divine will. This is a recurring theme among the Beguines for whom love means having the same will as God which is itself union.[35] The abandonment of personal, egotistical, will also includes abandoning the desire for virtue. The pursuit of the virtues can become a trap for the personal ego to take pride in itself, rather than lose itself in the contemplation of God. Marguerite, like the other Beguines, contrasts those who seek rewards from Love in the guise of unusual experiences such as visions or ecstasies, with those who love in a courtly fashion welcoming hardships and asking for no rewards, rather being willing even to be without love for love's sake. Marguerite is anxious to encourage souls beyond the selfish pursuit of virtue or ecstasy to the self-knowledge that reveals the soul to itself as the 'abyss of all poverty'.[36] Marguerite's insistence that the annihilated soul takes leave of the virtues formed one of the main points of the Inquisition against her, although she is at pains to explain that the soul must first pass through the virtues before being able to leave them behind.

The *Mirouer* is in two parts. The first 119 chapters consist of a series of dialogues between the soul and love on one side, and reason on the other. The last 20 chapters are almost entirely written in Marguerite's own 'voice', and may have been added after the book's initial condemnation and burning in Valenciennes. The *Mirouer* is unusual in comparison with the work of other mystics in that there is no nuptial imagery or use of the imagery of the Song of Songs. In this Marguerite resembles Hadewijch more than the other Beguine mystics. Nor is there any emphasis on the imaginative reliving of Christ's life on earth; indeed, Marguerite considers this a lower form of spirituality, rather like Mechtild who dismisses the suggestion that she rock the baby Jesus as a childish pleasure compared to her love of him.[37] Marguerite's discussion of the trinitarian economy of love suggests that she was familiar with scholastic trinitarian theology as well as Dionysian spirituality, which is an indication of the level of education that she must have enjoyed. As we have seen, Marguerite, like the other Beguines, draws on the literature of courtly love to illustrate her points and it seems probable that she, like them, gained her knowledge of courtly literature from her home background, rather than in the beguinage.

4. THE BEGUINES AND THE CHURCH

The previous chapters have shown that the Beguine movement was not of itself a movement of revolt against the established Church and its hierarchy. Some women were accused and even condemned of heresy, but to the extent that it is possible to ascertain what they actually believed the condemnations frequently appear to have been based on evidence that is open to benign interpretations as well. The women who became Beguines, especially in the first half of the thirteenth century, did so for reasons similar to those of the men who became Franciscans or Dominicans. They may have wished to dissociate themselves from the excesses of particular parish priests, but they had no desire to step outside the Church to do so. When, towards the end of the thirteenth century, there were increasing complaints that Beguines were refusing to accept communion from the hands of their parish priests, the core of the objection was that they were turning to the mendicant orders, not that they had turned away from the Church as a whole. This quarrel was in fact as much about the erosion of the power of the parish priest by the mendicant orders as it was about the Beguines themselves. The reputation for holiness of the Beguines ensured that other parishioners followed their lead in preferring the mendicants, and this preference showed itself not only on Sundays but also in the parishioners' last wills and testaments. Another indication that the Beguines did not consider themselves to be in revolt against the Church is the number of beguinages that joined the Cistercian and Benedictine Orders when it became possible to do so. Had the incumbents thought of themselves as in any way in revolt against the established Church they would not have embraced so enthusiastically the opportunity to join it.

Nor were the Beguines seeking to write innovative and shocking texts. Some of their apparently more startling and daring statements in fact reveal the influence of such establishment figures as Bernard of Clairvaux, Richard of St Victor and William of St Thierry. The innovation lay in their use of the vernacular to discuss matters previously only written of in Latin, and in their appropriation of certain images and themes. Writing in a very different context from the monastic theologians, it is scarcely surprising if their interpretation of images should differ in some respects from those who came before them. It is in the continuity they display with the monastic authorities who preceded them that the Beguines reveal most strongly their self-understanding as being part of an established tradition. For example, it is sometimes suggested that in their concentration on personal experience the Beguines are in some way evidence of a new, proto-Protestant way of thinking. On the contrary, they are consciously following the monastic tradition: Bernard of Clairvaux's third Sermon on the Song of Songs starts with the words 'Today we read in the book of experience', and he played an important role in emphasising the significance of a knowledge of self for an understanding of God, placing interiority at the centre of religion. He further refines the notion of experience by linking it with love – it is in the experience of loving that God can be known. God can only be approached through this experience, reason cannot penetrate the mystery. Speaking of such affective union with God, Bernard, like the Beguines after him, goes on to say that for the heart to be thus affected is no less than to become God. William of St Thierry, whose so-called 'Golden Epistle', the *Epistola ad Fratres de Monte Dei*, had a profound influence on the spirituality of the Beguines and others, similarly speaks of the knowledge of God that can be achieved only by love. This love is God-given, is indeed the love that is God, and only by means of that love can God be known. Another important influence on the spirituality of the

Beguines from the Church establishment was Richard of St Victor, particularly his text *De IV Gradibus Violentae Caritatis* (Of the Four Grades of Violent Love). Much in his description of love is similar to the startling language in Hadewijch and Beatrijs. He speaks of a love that wounds, binds and causes to sicken, and of the immensity of loving desire that cannot be satisfied – the more the soul receives, the more she desires – leading to a kind of madness.

The combination of the texts of highly trained monastic theologians and the experience of unschooled (in the sense of having little or no Latin) Beguines was an extremely fruitful one. Far from rejecting the ideas that formed part of the spiritual inheritance of the established Church, the Beguines absorbed them and made them their own. A similarly fruitful relationship characterised the relationship between the Beguines and the men who were their spiritual advisors, with both sides gaining insights from the interaction. Certainly later German mysticism owes much to Meister Eckhart's association with houses of Dominican nuns and Beguines, as well as with Marguerite Porete. The relationship between spiritual women and the male priests who came into contact with them, in some cases for very many years, was one potentially fraught with difficulty. The balance of power was unequal – the priest had the spiritual as well as the secular power, except that the woman was subtly outside the usual framework by virtue of her direct access to God in visions, other supernatural gifts, or her extraordinary virtue. In many cases, indeed I am sure one can say in most, the opportunities for manipulation, for exploitation, were never realised. The men served the women and gained spiritual nourishment from doing so. However, the relationship was also open to abuse and there is sufficient evidence to suggest that it was at times abused, that it is necessary to consider how it might be if all were not well with the relationship.

In the course of the thirteenth century the relationship changed in a number of subtle ways as new factors came into play. One of the roles of the priest and confessor which became increasingly important was to ensure that the woman in his charge remained orthodox, influencing the interpretation of her visions and discouraging her if her zeal threatened to take her thought in inappropriate directions. I would suggest for example that the careful formulations of doctrine of Mechtild of Magdeburg reveal the influence of male minders. The following paragraphs will look in more detail at three women who between them spanned the thirteenth century: Marie d'Oignies, Hadewijch, and Mechtild of Magdeburg, and the relationships they enjoyed with their spiritual directors.

Marie d'Oignies was born in 1177 and Jacques of Vitry wrote the *vita* which is how we know of her two years after her death in 1215. It is clear from the *vita* that the mystic woman was the dominant partner in the relationship. Jacques of Vitry accepts that God speaks directly through Marie and follows her advice. It is thought that he may have been speaking of himself when he relates the story of a priest who had two benefices but gave one up when Marie told him that God was offended by the riches and the prestige of the second benefice. The *vita* shows the Church and the universities (represented by Jacques himself) as humbled and willing to learn from a simple woman. The relationship between Marie and Jacques as revealed by the *vita* was one of mutual support and respect, even of love. However, the benefits flow predominantly one way – from Marie to Jacques. The similarity between her and the Cathars might have led to her being suspected of heresy, but in fact Jacques appears to have been convinced from the beginning of the orthodox nature of Marie's belief and of her life. He guided her and ensured her thinking remained orthodox, without ever denying the authority that came to her from God. She advised him, chastised him for faults she perceived in him and entered into long discussions with him on matters spiritual. The *vita* reveals the extent to which Jacques' knowledge of theological tradition, Church dogma and papal politics became blended with Marie's spiritual experiences in the course of their life together in Oignies.

The relationship he sketches for us is of the learned and

scholarly priest from Paris who comes to sit at the feet of the woman in Oignies, serving her as her mouthpiece, as the preacher she had prayed for from God. She, as a woman, was prevented from preaching to communicate to others what God had said to her, so she prayed for a preacher to be sent to her who could perform this function for her. In a very real sense, therefore, Jacques portrays himself as the servant of Marie.

Unlike the *vita* of Marie d'Oignies, we know Mechtild of Magdeburg principally through her own text, although, as we have seen, the text we have is based on a Latin version made by her confessor and the sequence of the texts probably reflects his ordering of the material not hers. Nevertheless, we come close here to having the voice of one of the spiritual women herself, rather than a biography written by a man with unashamedly his own agenda.

The figure of Mechtild's confessor, Heinrich von Halle, remains somewhat shadowy. It is uncertain when he became Mechtild's spiritual director. Indeed it is far from clear how Heinrich was able to fulfil this important role in her life, as the only information we have of him is that in 1246 he was lector in the Dominican house at Neuruppin, about 140 kilometers from Magdeburg. Presumably he took up some post in Magdeburg after that date. In 1271 he was in the Dominican house at Halle and died there not later than 1281. It has been suggested that the important spiritual guide of Mechtild's early years was not Heinrich von Halle, but Wichmann von Arnstein.[1] Wichmann spent many years in Magdeburg, initially as a Premonstratensian, then after 1230 as a Dominican, until 1246 when he moved to Neuruppin. He gained a reputation for holiness early on. It has even been suggested that he may have been the 'one person' whom Mechtild knew in Magdeburg.[2] However, it was Heinrich who encouraged Mechtild to write, and whose theological and political judgement enabled her to steer a course in the increasingly hazardous waters of the second half of the thirteenth century. He was the editor of her work until his death. After Mechtild's entry into the convent at Helfta it seems likely that his role diminished, although it has been suggested that the theological concerns of the seventh book, written in Helfta, may have been drawn from his teaching.

When Mechtild first went to Magdeburg, the Beguines were being hailed as the holiest of the new religious movements. At the time of her death they were coming under increasing criticism and suspicion of heresy. As we have seen, her book reflects an acute awareness of the spiritual dangers surrounding Beguines in the world. She quotes her confessor on more than one occasion and the vehemence with which she repudiates certain heretical opinions strikes a rather contrived note, suggesting that they may have been inserted following the advice of her spiritual director with a view to pre-empting criticism. She stresses that a Beguine's first temporal duty is obedience to her spiritual advisor. This, she suggests, is the only way a Beguine has of preserving herself from heresy.

Mechtild shows much respect for the Church, especially for the Dominican Order, but that respect does not obscure for her the real faults she sees around her, and her critical voice enables us to catch a glimpse of some of the realities of life as a Beguine. Some of Mechtild's most vivid descriptions of hell are reserved for wicked or hypocritical priests. For example, she describes how the souls of those priests 'who burned here with greed and lasciviousness' float like fish in the boiling metal of purgatory to be caught by devils with fiery claws, boiled and eaten. She was also clearly aware of occasions when the obedience demanded by priests and confessors was obedience to their wills rather than to that of God. She describes a vision she has had of the soul of a Dominican brother killed by lightning. He appears to Mechtild in heavenly bliss, though not yet in heaven, with a stain on his face. When asked the cause of this stain he explains that it is caused by his tendency to be stern with those who did not do his will.

Hadewijch will have been a contemporary of Mechtild's, but unlike Mechtild, she hardly ever mentions clergy or the Church in specific or general terms. So in this area, as in so many others, we are once again dependent on the gleanings of tangential remarks and chance comments in the endeavour to penetrate behind the texts of Hadewijch's work to the reality of her life.

It seems likely that Hadewijch too had a particular affection and respect for the Dominican Order. This can be inferred from her praise for Mary Magdalene, the patron of the Order of Preachers, in the third of her Mengeldichten where she describes her as the example to be followed above all others on account of her love. However, in marked contrast to Mechtild, there is no indication that she was under a spiritual director, or that she took pains that her visions or observations should be understood to be completely orthodox. Where she does make a remark about the clergy it is generally a criticism of hypocritical priests or of those lacking in spirituality.

The List of the Perfect Ones at the end of the Visions is the only source of what might be termed biographical data and even that is thin and possibly suspect – it is assumed that Hadewijch wrote it, but there is no evidence other than a correspondence with other texts ascribed to her. From the List it would appear that she had a close relationship with at least one monk. She writes: 'Honorius who lay on a rock in the sea is the twenty-fourth [perfect one], to whom I sent a monk who was used to visit me often.' It is rather hard to reconcile the idea of a monk, with vows of stability, with the image of an intrepid voyager to a rock in the sea, although this may have been no more than an island in an estuary. From the rest of the List it appears that some of Hadewijch's visitors came in the spirit – that is, in a kind of visionary experience. Her description of the man as a monk suggests that she may have sent him to visit Honorius in the spirit, in which case his regular visits to her may have been in the spirit too. Another person mentioned in the List who may have been a cleric is Lord Hendric of Breda whom she sent to visit a hermit or anchoress in Saxony. There has been a great deal of speculation about who this man might have been; unfortunately the family trees of the noble families which could possibly lay claim to the epithet 'of Breda' have yielded no clue. One possibility is

that he was a cleric and that once again Hadewijch was referring to a journey made in the spirit. Whether her relationship
with these priests was in the spirit or in the flesh, as it were,
the Hadewijch texts clearly show that as far as the author was
concerned, she was able to give them directions. Nowhere do
the texts suggest that she perceived herself as subordinate to
anyone but God.

In all this Hadewijch is in marked contrast to Mechtild.
From her texts one gets the impression rather of a woman
such as Marie d'Oignies than of a Beguine aware of criticism
and of the looming power of the stake. It would not be right
to seek to date Hadewijch on the basis of her apparent indiffer-
ence to the possibility of criticism; after all, one of the features
of Marguerite Porete's book *The Mirror of Simple Souls* is her
outspoken criticism of the Church regardless of the consequences. Nevertheless, this is yet another small piece to add
to the picture that Hadewijch was active in the first part of
the century rather than the second.

Another source of information about the role of male spiritual advisors in the lives of the Beguines are the *vitae* of
the women themselves. These tended to be written by their
confessors or by others on the basis of the confessor's testi-
mony, and therefore require careful interpretation in the light
of their own agenda. As the thirteenth century progressed,
the confidants of the Beguines were increasingly Dominicans.[3]
This was at times against the wishes of the Order itself, but
seems always to have been eagerly sought by the individual
Dominicans. The *vitae* reveal a fascination, at times an almost
prurient obsession, with the more unusual features of the
women's lives. For example, Peter of Dacia, the friend and
confidant of the Beguine Christine of Stommeln (1242–1312),
records in bizarre detail events such as when a demon defe-
cated on her in his presence, and repeatedly asks her to write
to him with information about the demons' behaviour towards
her.

The *vitae* suggest that over time the relationship between
the Dominicans and the spiritual women over whom they had

charge changed. The life of Margaret of Ypres (d. 1237) suggests that her confessor Siger of Lille, who had been
responsible for her original conversion, continued to have
authority over her until her death. Other Dominicans are
shown to have gone to spiritual women for prayers in much
the same way as Jacques of Vitry shows himself to have bene-
fited from the prayers of Marie d'Oignies. Thomas of
Cantimpre, for example, asks the Beguine Lutgard of Aywieres
to pray for him to be released from temptation when he heard
confession. In later *vitae*, such as those of Christine of Stommeln and of the Italian tertiary Benvenuta Boiani (1255–92),
the role of the friars is shown as less unambiguously authori-
tarian than in that of Margaret of Ypres. The women give the
friars privileged access to the divine and they see their charges
as objects of devotion as well as, or even instead of, objects of
direction. The difficult question of the relationship between
the authority of the friars as priests and that of the women
conferred by their direct access to the divine does not appear
to be at issue. The most harmonious relationship between the
priest and his spiritual charge can be found in the *vita* of
Catherine of Sienna (1347–80) written by her confessor
Raymond of Capua (d. 1399). Here her charismatic power
works for and together with his power as priest for the benefit
of the Church and Christian salvation. Coakley describes the
relationship in the *vita* as follows: 'Here we have the most
harmonious and ambitious male vision of the female saint, in
the sense that her powers complement those of the Church
and she and Raymond form together a sort of androgynous
unit for the salvation of Christendom.'[4] Later *vitae* show the
saint and priest working quite separately, so the relationship
described by Raymond may have been due to the personalities
of those involved rather than any real development.

This survey of relationships between spiritual women and
their male confidants shows that relationships changed in the
course of the century. In some cases the spirituality and supernatural gifts of the women gave them a unique authority and
like the sibyls of old they were sought as sources of advice

and guidance by men. In these cases their male confessors and confidants were responsible for their material security and support, rather than their spiritual safety. In other cases women were relying on them for spiritual guidance, and on the fact that they were known to have confessors and spiritual directors to save them from accusations of heresy. These changes may have depended on the people concerned as much or more than on external conditions. For example, the relationship between Siger of Lille and Margaret of Ypres is closely contemporaneous with that between Mechtild of Magdeburg and Heinrich of Halle, but whereas Siger is shown as having clear authority over Margaret, this is less true of Mechtild and Heinrich. Although Mechtild appreciates his presence as a protection against accusations of heresy and his wisdom as a guide to remaining orthodox, she retains a greater degree of independence than that attributed to Margaret. This may be an example of the influence of authorship on the account. It is interesting that the texts by women in the latter half of the thirteenth century suggest that they valued their confessors as insurance against accusations of heresy, whereas the *vitae* written by men speak only of their veneration of the women as in receipt of special divine grace, perhaps because the authors of the *vitae* were keen to emphasise the undoubted orthodoxy of their charges.

5. BRIDES IN THE DESERT: KEY IMAGES IN BEGUINE SPIRITUALITY

BRIDAL/NUPTIAL IMAGERY

The imagery most frequently associated with medieval women mystics is that described as 'bridal mysticism'. Some critics perceive this imagery to be uniquely appropriate to women, forgetting that its roots go back to Plotinus and beyond. Furthermore, the use mystics, men as well as women, made of it was greatly influenced by the example of Bernard of Clairvaux. The frequency of bridal or nuptial imagery is sometimes seen as evidence for repressed sexual feelings and even perversion, with little consideration of the range of imagery that falls into that category, or the historical and cultural context. Without wishing to fall into the same error of making blanket assertions in reverse, there is something rather simplistic about the view that all nuptial imagery must necessarily reveal some sexual perversion. Our age, especially post-Freud, is far more obsessed by sexuality than previous ages were. Even today it is recognised that the sex-drive is far stronger in some individuals than in others, so even at this crude level it is possible to postulate that some of the mystics may have had less need to repress their sexuality than others. To suppose that all those who used such imagery were subconsciously fulfilling a personal need ignores the extent to which this imagery was an accepted and even respected element of the cultural climate. When casting around for a suitable image or metaphor to express their experience, the medieval mystic will not have been driven by the urge for originality which drives twentieth-century authors. They will have been happy to make use of established imagery, in much the same way that we might casually say of someone who acted well under pressure 'she was as cool as a cucumber', without giving any particular thought to the characteristics of cucumbers or our feelings about them – we are simply using an image which has common currency in order to describe a situation.

Attentive reading of the texts shows that there are considerable variations within what one might take to be the broad category of 'bridal mysticism'. Mystics of both sexes have drawn on the relationship between a man and a woman for some of their most powerful imagery, but the essence of a mystic's vision is less the category of images they choose than what they do with the images they have chosen. Image language is rich in meaning because it arouses echoes in its readers. The relationship between two lovers is the most intimate and intense of human relationships – even more so than that between parent and child. And when the lovers are a man and a woman, to this intimacy is added the extraordinary fact of otherness. The relationship between a man and a woman, between a lover and his mistress, is one between two beings that are in many quite fundamental ways 'other'. In this way too, the imagery is an appropriate one for the relationship between God and his creatures.

Bernard of Clairvaux perceived the importance of this notion of 'otherness' in the relationship between God and the soul, and used the imagery of the Song of Songs to underline it. Speaking to an audience of men who had entered the cloister as adults (the Cistercian Order was the first to refuse child oblates), Bernard used the sensuous language of the Song of Songs as an allegory of the relationship between their souls and God. By speaking of their souls as the brides of Christ, Bernard emphasised the fact that the relationship was both like and yet totally unlike any other relationship they had ever experienced. They might have been married or enjoyed amorous encounters before their conversion, but in none of them would they have been a woman. This underlying awareness of dislocation is naturally absent from texts written by women drawing on this same imagery. Furthermore, as we saw earlier, the apparent dichotomy 'man is to woman as soul is to body' combined with the related sentiment that man was the Divinity of Christ and woman his humanity to give women a special position in relation to God and to the incarnation. To speak of man as the Divinity of Christ was clearly metaphorical; but to speak of woman as being his humanity was in some sense literally true. In other words, there was a sense in which the soul as bride really was woman, sinful flesh, not merely an allegory for her, so when speaking of it in this way a woman was speaking of reality.

When developing the image of the soul as the bride of Christ, the language and imagery used by Bernard and other men is heavily derivative of the Bible, while the Beguines who used this image appear to draw more on contemporary situations, making it their own, speaking more clearly of the feminine experience. From the pages of Mechtild of Magdeburg's 'Flowing light of the Godhead', for example, comes a picture of an established, warm, marital relationship between her soul and its spouse as the lord and lady of a castle.[1] Not for her just the longings of the bride in the Song of Songs, there is a warmth and an affectionate intimacy in the relationship she portrays which are absent in Bernard. The greater three-dimensionality, warmth and realism in the relationship sketched by Mechtild may well be attributable to the fact that she was drawing from life in a way that Bernard was not. The use by men of nuptial imagery to speak of their souls involved an imaginative inversion from an active role to a passive one, and from a position of power as men to one of weakness as a woman. For a woman to speak of herself imaginatively as the bride of the Son of God requires the inversion of only one aspect of the courtly love myth, namely that the woman is of a superior status to her lover.

However, not all the Beguines wrote in this way. Hadewijch, for example, imported the notion of otherness achieved by gender reversal into her texts, especially her poetry. She, a woman, speaks of herself as a man in relation to God, a noble lady. In the same way that the feminine gender of the Latin noun for soul, *anima*, helped the development of the Song of Songs as the prime allegory of the soul's relationship to God, Hadewijch may have been inspired by the feminine gender of the Dutch noun for love, *minne*. In the context of Hadewijch's imagery, that of courtly love, it is the woman who enjoys the power whereas the humble knight is powerless. She underlines on several occasions the paradox of her speech, drawing attention to the fact that she is a woman, thereby emphasising the otherness of the relationship she describes. As with the relationships in conventional courtly love poems and romances, the lover-knight needs all his courage to win the favours of his changeable and exacting lady and to withstand the pain and disappointments of the trials along the way. The trials are all made worthwhile by the promise of delights once the lady's favour has been won. Love describes the delights in store for the one who wins her favours in sensual terms:

> 'I will warm you
> I am that I was before.
> Now fall into my arms
> and enjoy my generous teaching.'
>
> (Poem in Stanzas 20: refrain)

The relationship between God and the soul which Hadewijch describes is very far from the standard patriarchal relationship currently decried by feminists and others. However, it would be wrong to interpret this as evidence of feminist theology *avant la lettre*. During the Middle Ages the notion of gender and gender difference was much more fluid than it is today. It is not unusual for there to be gender shifts between texts and even within the same text. Hadewijch, for example, in one poem describes Love both as the noble mistress for whom the lover-knight must willingly risk everything, and who rightly demands absolute loyalty and obedience with no thought for any reward or recompense, and as the opposing knight in a tournament who does not fight fair and whom one must endeavour to overcome.[2] Male and female were seen as the ends of a continuum, more certainly joined by the fact of being creatures before God than divided by their sexual differences. There is therefore a danger that we, with our post-Freudian mind-set, will interpret medieval texts in quite anachronistic ways, that we will see significance in juxtapositions which would have been considered entirely without significance at the time of composition. To suggest that Hadewijch was making a proto-feminist statement by speaking of God in this way is to ignore the occasions when she speaks of God as a feudal lord or as a knight in battle – such simplification does justice neither to the subtlety of Hadewijch's thought nor to feminist theology.

The forty-five Poems in Stanzas are one of the most remark-able poetic achievements in the Dutch language. Hadewijch has taken the form and conventions of the French courtly love lyric and transposed them into Dutch, and from secular to religious love. The gender reversal she employs (speaking of herself and her audience as a man) enables her to illustrate as well as simply describe the fact that the relationship between God and the soul is completely 'other' – it is like nothing her audience has ever experienced before. Many of the Beguines will have been wives and mothers and have been courted with poetry like that being read to them, but in none of these relationships will they have been the man, the lover-knight. In the ninth Poem in Stanzas she describes the knight as follows:

A handsome mien, fine clothes
And fine language adorn the knight;
To suffer all for Love without bitterness
Is a handsome mien for those who can do it;
His clothes are then his actions,
Performed with new ardour and without complacency
And more ready to help strangers in every need
Than his own friends;
That is colour, these tokens of nobility
Count most highly in Love's eyes.

(Poem in Stanzas 9:31–40)

She develops the martial image to draw the attention of her audience to behaviour appropriate for the knightly lovers of Love. It is important not to show what one is suffering – that is the significance of her emphasis on the handsome mien or appearance of the knight. The reference to colour is significant as the wearing of colours other than brown and shades of buff was restricted to specific classes, aristocratic and patrician, during the Middle Ages. Elsewhere, the fiction enables her to speak more fully of the sacrifices required in the service of God and of the divine, and of the unswerving, single-minded devotion in the midst of suffering and confusion required of the loyal servants. Other Beguines, such as Mechtild of Magdeburg for example, drawing on the imagery of courtly love, have spoken of themselves in the *persona* of the loyal *amie*, but here Hadewijch goes further and takes on an even more active role. For Hadewijch the relationship with God demands courage, dedication and endurance.

The *Fliessende Licht der Gottheit* (Flowing Light of the Godhead) is not, as we have said, a reliable guide to the spiritual development of Mechtild of Magdeburg, following as it does the programme set out by her in Book 7:3: 'Your childhood was the playmate of my Holy Spirit, your youth the bride of my humanity, and now your old age is the mistress of the house of my Divinity.'[3] In the early books the soul is portrayed as a sleeping maiden whom love must awake and urge to love and follow Christ:

> Love: Alas foolish soul, where are you?
> . . .
> Soul: Do not awaken me
> I do not know what you are saying.
> Love: One must awaken the queen
> when the king desires to come to her.
> Soul: I am in a holy order
> I fast, I keep vigils, I am without mortal sin
> I am sufficiently bound.
>
> . . .

> How can I love so gladly someone
> Whom I do not know?
> Love: Alas how can you not recognize the Lord
> Who is named so often to you?
>
> . . .
>
> Ah beloved let me awaken you.
>
> (Book 2:23)

Having been awakened by love, in a subsequent vision God describes the soul as follows:

> You are like a new bride,
> whose only love has left her sleeping
> from whom she cannot bear to part for even one hour . . .
> I await you in the orchard of love
> And pick for you the flower of sweet reunion
> And make ready there your bed.

The soul replies:

> Ah my beloved, I am hoarse in the throat of my chastity
> But the sweetness of your kindness
> Has cleared my throat so that now I can sing.
>
> (Book 2:25)

In later books she is described as the mistress of the house:

> The soul and the flesh is at home in heaven and sits with the eternal host whom it resembles, the host honouring the lady of the house at his side. The lords and serving knights are the holy angels. All the service they offer is dedicated to the host and the lady of the house. (Book 4:14)

In light of earlier observations about the way women appropriated the language of the flesh as peculiarly their own, it is important to note that soul and body are together at home in heaven. Today we tend to interpret the dichotomy 'man is to woman as soul is to body' as reflecting a very negative view of women. However, for Mechtild and many of the other Beguines both soul and body were inseparable parts of the whole (wo)man. The same point is made again in a later book where in a vision the virtues describe themselves as follows:

> We are noble and well-bred maidens
> Who serve to glorify God
> In his best beloved Queen
> Whom God has chosen above all
> namely the human soul and body.

(Book 7:62)

A popular image of medieval piety was that of nursing the Christ Child.[4] Mechtild, however, remarks almost contemptuously:

> That is a childish joy,
> To suckle and rock a babe!
> But I am a full-grown bride,
> I must to my lover's side.

(Book 1:44)

As we shall see when we consider the attitude of these women to suffering, for Mechtild the bed on which she lies beside her lover is characterised by pain, not joyful pleasure. Unalloyed pleasure she describes as childish and her reference to being full-grown is a reference to being willing to embrace the suffering that is part, if not the essence, of union.

SUFFERING

Like the images they choose to use to speak of God, the attitude of these mystic women to suffering is individual and distinctive. They illustrate the range of attitudes possible within Christianity: suffering in the context of *imitatio Christi*; suffering in order to release others from the consequences of sin; as the necessary preparation of the soul for union with God; as the *locus* of that union. In the late twentieth century, suffering, like death, has become for us what sex was to the Victorians – a subject to be ignored as much as possible, not referred to in conversation (polite or otherwise) and those who are tainted by it to be shunned like medieval lepers. Because we are now able to suppress so much pain, to remove those suffering incurable diseases to the safe distance of hospitals and nursing homes, there is a tendency to see the medieval woman's awareness of suffering and her efforts to make sense of that which she sees all around her as somehow perverted or pathological. When considering the attitudes to suffering we should not lose our historical sense: in the Middle Ages suffering was not so easy to ignore as it is now. There were no painkillers; damp and insanitary housing meant that if you were lucky enough to survive into adulthood you would probably not do so without illness and pain. Death and the loss of loved ones was a daily reality – one in five births resulted in the death of the mother. There is no evidence to support the extraordinary assertion that medieval parents did not care as much about their children as we do today. There were good, devoted parents then as now and the epitaphs on graves, or the evidence in letters, show how deeply even the death of a new baby was felt.[5]

The inclination to provoke suffering (for example, by excessive fasting or drinking dirty water), which has been seen as a feature of female spirituality, is not as common an occurrence in this period as it was to become later. It is worthy of note that those early women mystics whose own texts we have, for example Hildegard of Bingen and Hadewijch, are unequivocal in their condemnation of excessive asceticism amounting to self-harm. Descriptions of such practices are confined to the *vitae* of holy women, mostly written by men. With all hagiography there is more than an element of authors inserting into the story aspects which they feel should have been there; it is therefore arguable that the tales of extreme asceticism reflect not what women did but what their male confessors thought was appropriate. For women in subsequent centuries this kind of behaviour will have been part of their mystic role model and subconsciously or consciously they will have sought to emulate what they perceived as the example of their predecessors, thereby confirming the (male) view of appropriate behaviour. In fact none of the great mystics demonstrate the abhorrence of the body evidenced by the practices described in early *vitae* and those of later mystics. For Hadewijch it is only by being in the body, by being flesh, and sharing unequivocally the humanity of Christ, that it is possible to be one with him. The attitudes to suffering which these women describe are attempts to make sense of suffering which can not be avoided and which they see all around them. To speak of suffering as a means of atoning for the sins of others does not refer to self-inflicted suffering, rather it presents a way of accepting and living with the suffering which was a natural part of their lives. For these women, for whom the dichotomy 'man is Christ's divinity and woman his humanity' was a lived reality, a woman's suffering patiently borne was in some real sense the suffering of Christ.

For Mechtild of Magdeburg, suffering is an integral part of her relationship with God. Of that relationship the soul is described as saying:

> 'I am his joy; he is my suffering.'
>
> (Book 1:5)

On another occasion the soul speaks to God as follows:

> Lord, what shall we now say of love?
> Now that we lie so close on the bed of my pain.
>
> (Book 7:21)

It is also that which prepares the soul for the relationship. Pain and suffering are described as the bridal clothes of the soul, not taken off after marriage.[6]

Mechtild describes the acceptance of suffering as a healthful spiritual drink. She writes:

> I am ailing and I yearn for a healthful drink
>   . . .
> this drink means suffering for love of God.
> The pain is bitter
> And so we mix it with an herb called 'suffering gladly'

> The second herb is called 'patience in pain'
> And it too is bitter
> Therefore we add another herb 'holy devotion'
> Which renders patience and all our work sweet.
>
> . . .
>
> Ah dear Lord if you gave me this to drink
> I would live undaunted and joyfully in pain
> I would forfeit for a while the Kingdom of Heaven
> So great is my yearning for it.
>
> (Book 7:33)

The drink is described as being that which Christ drank when he came to earth and which intoxicated him with fiery love. The attitude to pain illustrated here is not one of maudlin sentimentality. Mechtild sees clearly that to suffer for love of God (whether this is interpreted as being made to suffer by others on account of one's love for God, or the acceptance of physical suffering as an offering of love to God) is an experience of bitter pain. Even patience in pain is bitter and the drink needs to be sweetened by holy devotion in order to make it palatable. But her desire for the drink is so great that she would postpone entry into the Kingdom of Heaven in order to savour it longer.[7]

For Hadewijch the drink is not described as sweetened by herbs. Speaking of Lady Love – *minne* – she writes:

> She (*Minne*) is generous too
> and pours full measure
> but those who drink with her
> she causes to pay in blood.
>
> (Mengeldicht 24:74–96)

This image is of itself a very powerful one, but it is made even more striking by Hadewijch's punning use of homonyms. This literary device, which works very well in poetry which was to be listened to rather than read, is a favourite technique of Hadewijch's which she uses to create paradoxes and what Annemarie Schimmel has described as the intellectual shock therapy favoured by mystics in order to induce their listeners to a supra-logical understanding.[8] In this poem Hadewijch uses the verb *scinken* which means 'to pour' but which can also mean 'to cause pain'. The lines can therefore also be translated as follows:

> She (*Minne*) is generous too
> and causes full measure of pain:
> those who drink with her
> she causes to pay in blood.

Suffering is for both Mechtild and Hadewijch also the means to union. Mechtild writes: 'I will and must drink from the same cup as my Father if I am to posses him richly' (Book 7:52). But for Hadewijch, as we have seen, suffering is not just the means to union, it is the *locus* of union itself. For her, suffering is not purely physical – she speaks especially of spiritual suffering endured because of the growing awareness of the absence of the Loved One. In her visions and letters she repeatedly stresses the necessity of suffering with Christ as man on earth rather than just desiring to enjoy union with his godhead. In her letters she speaks of the need to carry the cross with Christ, and not with Simon who was paid to do so. The payment Hadewijch has in mind for her fellow Beguines is experiences of ecstatic union, visions and the like. To suffer in order to receive such 'payment' is not to suffer as Christ suffered. The desire for ecstasies, visions and other phenomena is considered a sign of spiritual immaturity by all the Beguines. Marguerite Porete speaks scathingly of those who expect large revenues from love, dismissing them as asses or sheep who seek to save themselves 'in a far from courtly manner' (*Mirouer*, chapter 62).

The Beguines' opinions may have been coloured by their own experience as all these women appear to have had visionary experiences and ecstasies early in their careers, followed by a more quiet period. For many people even today such experiences are seen as signs of special grace, indicative of a high degree of favour with God. Hadewijch, however, reflects the general scepticism of the other Beguines when she suggests that visions are by no means necessarily indicative of grace. She describes how God may give such experiences early on to encourage souls, but makes clear that these favours are just the first stage of a long and hard road. They are among the childish things of which Paul speaks and which need to be put away as the soul progresses. It seems likely that Hadewijch herself went through a long period without any visions or any other similar indications of God's favour, and this helped her realise that the depth and richness of the relationship with God illustrated by visionary experiences is insignificant compared with that reached through suffering.

For Hadewijch the highest form of union with God is that within and by means of the agonising experience of his absence. In her thirteenth vision Hadewijch is shown the various stages on the approach to God, to *minne*. As we have seen, the eighth and highest way is to realise that the closest one can get to God is in the suffering caused by the awareness of his absence. The soul's desire for God becomes ever greater in unfaith and it is in the greatness of this unfulfilled love that the soul is able to become one with the love that is God. Love is the means and the place of union. This union resembles that which St Teresa of Avila describes as the highest kind – the permanent union which does not prevent strenuous activity by plunging the mystic into trances or ecstatic states. Rather it is part of the daily awareness of the mystic which suffuses all she (or he) does. There has been much theological debate as to whether such a permanent state of union is possible this side of heaven. Defined as Hadewijch and the other Beguines do, it clearly is and is quite different from a state of bliss in heaven, however one might seek to define that.

For Hadewijch the pain and suffering of human exile is the place of closest encounter with God. Many today are inclined to see pain or suffering as wholly negative and even as a punishment. For the Beguines, however, suffering is not a sign of divine wrath, and could even be a signal sign of God's favour.

Mechtild describes God as saying to her: 'Your life is sanctified because my rod has never left your back' (Book 7:4).

DESERT

In poetic texts, as we have seen, image language is used as a kind of shorthand, a way of evoking a whole range of experience and of bringing to mind a wide range of concepts. Images are used to evoke a series of affective responses from the audience with little or no discursive explanation. Images may be drawn from experience or from religious or literary sources, and different sources may lead to different uses of apparently the same image. The sources of the imagery of the desert that were particularly powerful for monastic theologians, such as for example Richard of St Victor, were the passages in Numbers speaking of the children of Israel wandering in the desert before entering the Promised Land. Life on earth was interpreted as a form of exile during which the soul tries constantly to return to its home with God. The biblical passage was seen as a *figura* of the monastic life, and of the soul's journey towards God. The desert was, however, the place of Moses' encounter with God and another source is the verse in Hosea where the desert is described as the solitude wherein God speaks to the soul: 'Therefore, behold, I will allure her, and bring her into the wilderness, and speak comfortably unto her' (Hosea 2:14). These two sources inevitably lead to very different implications of the desert image – the first presents the desert as a time of waiting and of trial, the second as the *locus* of encounter with God.[9]

We know that Hadewijch was familiar with the work of Richard of St Victor, and in respect of her use of the image of the desert she is writing clearly within the monastic tradition.

> Now may God assist those
> who would gladly give satisfaction
> According to love's wishes

> And struggle through the deep desert
> to the land of love
>
> (Poem in Stanzas 36:133–7)

The desert is here a place to be crossed with difficulty. The verb *dorewaden* is a cognate of the English verb *to wade* and gives the impression of forging a path where there is none. If we look at Hadewijch's other uses of the word *wuestine* in the Poems in Stanzas this impression is reinforced.

> It is an incomprehensible wonder
> that has bound my heart
> And causes [me] to wander in a wild wilderness;
> Such a cruel desert was never created
> As love can make in her country
> Because she causes [us] to long for her with desire
> And to taste her being without knowledge.
>
> (Poem in Stanzas 22:26–30)

Here the verb *dolen*, 'to wander', associated with the passage in Numbers, clearly evokes the experience of the people of Israel in the desert. With its implications of being lost, of fear and uncertainty, the word also expands the sense of difficulty created in the previous quotation. The subsequent description of the desert as cruel, combined with the use of the modal verb *can*, suggests that the desert and the difficulties therein are imposed by *minne*. This reinforces the impression of the modal verb *doen* two lines previously in the phrase *doen dolen*, 'causes me to wander'. The wider imaginative context of *minne's* imposition of the desert is an echo of God's decision that the people of Israel should wander a further forty years in the desert before entering the Promised Land they had glimpsed. In light of Hadewijch's own life, her early visionary and ecstatic experiences followed by a lengthy period when all such favours had deserted her, this could be a *figura* for her experience of the mystic life. She goes on to define the desert in the last lines quoted as the experience of desire for *minne* and of having a taste of her being without further knowledge.

This has an interesting parallel in Mengeldicht 19 which is discussed below.

Hadewijch describes the Promised Land as the land of plenty:

> You shall row through all storms
> Until you come to that land of plenty
> Where the lover and the beloved shall flow through all;
> Of that noble faithfulness is your surety here [on earth].
>
> (Poem in Stanzas 4:45–8)

It is interesting to see that here the ocean and its storms have briefly taken the place of the desert as the locus of trial – an indication perhaps of the role of experience in the choice of images as Hadewijch was a member of a seafaring nation where the main transport routes were (and still are) rivers huge by European standards. The surety of the promise of reaching the Promised Land is faithful service here on earth despite all the trials along the way. The Promised Land is characterised by an abundance of flowing mutual love not unlike the activity within the Trinity, thereby underlining the fact that it represents ultimate union with God. It is worth noting in this context that another meaning of the verb *dorevloyen* is 'to fill to overflowing', 'to satisfy completely'.

Elsewhere the Promised Land is also associated with wideness and openness:

> He who desires to embrace the wide extent of love
> He shall understand love
> . . .
> She reveals her extent, her highest abode
> – Take note everyone –
> Only to him who has given satisfaction
> with his suffering
> in love.
>
> (Poem in Stanzas 36:23–4, 29–33)

The Promised Land is only obtainable by means of suffering in love, the trials of the desert described above. In order to embrace, and to be embraced by, the fullness of love, the wideness of the Promised Land, the soul must itself be expanded.

> I wish to devote all my time
> To noble consideration of great love
> Because she with her great power
> Makes my being so wide.
>
> (Poem in Stanzas 31:1–4)

It is the power of *minne* that widens the lover's nature in preparation for the Promised Land. Later in the same poem Hadewijch refers to the process as learning the ways (literally roads) of love. Although the desert is a place of anxiety and uncertainty, it is *minne* herself that leads the way, teaching the road to follow. The imaginative context is the experience of the people of Israel condemned by God to wander in the desert but led by him by the pillars of smoke and of fire.

Hadewijch is writing within the tradition of monastic theology when she employs the image of the desert and of the children of Israel's wandering before entry into the Promised Land as a *figura* for a life dedicated to God. It is *minne* that creates the desert as a place of trial and preparation before entry into the Promised Land can be attained and paradoxically it is *minne* also that shows the way. Hadewijch has appropriated images familiar in a monastic, primarily masculine, context to reinforce the lay women in her circle in the mystic life they have chosen. In the Mengeldichten 17–24 there is explicit reference to the passage in Numbers describing the wandering of the tribe of Israel in the wilderness. Four stanzas are devoted to the incident where Moses sends Joshua and Caleb to explore the Promised Land.

> Even though those who are arid
> In faith
> Remain without surety,
> Hasten forward
> And make your way through
> Into that fat land.

It is such:
There flows honey and milk
That is clear to those
Who searched within
And with three fruits
Came thence

And carried them
To where those of Israel saw
The noble goods;
But they had no more taste nor smell of it
Even though it lay before them
Than [had they had only] a report.

(Mengeldicht 18:313–30)

The Promised Land of union with God is explicitly drawn from the biblical source as a land flowing with milk and honey. In this context it is interesting to note that Richard of St Victor interprets milk as symbolic of the humanity of Christ and honey as symbolic of his divinity. The stanza is further loaded with meaning by the trinitarian reference to three fruits and the use of the word 'within' which could refer both to the Promised Land and to the soul. Like Hadewijch, this poet sees the desert as a spiritual, psychological landscape.

Progress into the Promised Land is described with verbs of movement. The poet urges her audience, 'Hasten forwards and make your way through into the land of plenty' (Mengeldicht 18:331–6), and later observes, 'But he who goes forward receives that noble possession of which he who stands still knows nothing but rumours' (Mengeldicht 18:331–6). In contrast to this movement, the desert is associated with those who stand still:

Knowledge escapes me [I am]
beyond understanding and
far beyond sense.
Therefore I must be silent

> and still remain
> where I am.
>
> But it resembles a desert
> to be there
> in this way
> because there neither
> sense nor word
> can obtain or achieve anything.
>
> (Mengeldicht 19:88–96)

Like Hadewijch in Poem in Stanzas 22, the desert is defined as having no more knowledge of the Promised Land than had the children of Israel following the reports of Joshua and Caleb.

Elsewhere the poet speaks of the process of preparation for entry into the Promised Land of union with God, describing it as one of being both led and broadened. As for Hadewijch, it is the power of *minne* that effects the necessary transformation:

> With the power of love
> thought must
> from herself
> be wrest,
> and forcibly turned
> to the transcendent.
>
> There she will be led,
> purged, enlarged
> in obscure ways
> and be raised up
> into a noble existence
> as the triumph of grace.
>
> (Mengeldicht 18:7–18)

Thought needs to be wrenched away from itself and focused on the transcendent. There it will be led along hidden paths and expanded until by grace it is resurrected to new life. All this is the work of love and of grace. If these lines are compared to those quoted above from Poem in Stanzas 31, the similarities in the poets' frames of reference are striking.

The Mengeldichten 25–29 may or may not be by a single author. There are clear stylistic similarities between poems 25 and 27, but the others are different both from each other and from the other Mengeldichten. The one direct reference to the desert occurs in poem 28. This poem is a lament about the fickle behaviour of *minne*, and in the final stanza the poet writes:

> You are mean and noble,
> Soft as a lamb, and savage
> As untamed wild animals
> In the desert without moderation.
>
> (Mengeldicht 28:21–4)

The last line is somewhat ambiguous; it could be descriptive of the animals referred to in the previous line, or it could be a reference to the location of the totality of the experience. In neither case is there reference to the passage from Numbers as the wider context. The poet rather appears to locate the entire encounter with *minne* in the desert.

The other poem in this collection which is of interest in this context is poem 26. The poet never uses the word *woestine* (wilderness or desert) but speaks of the *weelde wide eenuldicheit* (the wild wide simplicity). This is the place where the poor in spirit, those whom the Beatitudes describe as seeing God, live in unity:

> In this wild wide simplicity
> Live the poor in spirit in unity.
> There they find nothing but emptiness
> Which always responds to eternity.
>
> (Mengeldicht 26:25–8)

The poet describes the desert as being without end or beginning, without form and without rational thought. The poor in spirit must be free from all things – from images and from other creatures – in order to live there. She acknowledges that reaching this goal is not easy:

> This was said in few words
> But their way is long, that I know well.
> For they must suffer many ills
> Who prove this fully once and for all.
>
> (Mengeldicht 26:29–32)

Here, even more than in poem 28, the *figura* of the children of Israel wandering the desert before entering into the Promised Land has faded from view. The notion of the desert responding to eternity recalls the line in Psalm 41:8, 'abyssus abyssum invocat', which is also important in Hadewijch's spiritual theology. She, however, uses the word *afgrond* (literally abyss). For her as for Beatrijs of Nazareth the abyss, unlike the desert, is the *locus* of encounter with God. The most striking difference between the desert in this poem and that in texts by Hadewijch and in the Mengeldichten 17–24 is that here the desert has become the goal. The sufferings are endured on the way to the desert, not, as in the other texts, in the desert on the way to the Promised Land.

Mechtild of Magdeburg's book, the *Fliessende Licht der Gottheit*, was written over a long period, and it is probable that, when writing her book, her early experiences were filtered through those later in her life when Beguines were coming under increasing criticism and suspicion of heresy. Although some of her visions were earlier than others, many reflect the perspective of Beguine spirituality towards the later part of the century.

Of the desert Mechtild writes:

The Desert has Twelve Characteristics

> You shall love the nothing,
> You shall flee from the something,
> You shall stand alone,
> And go to no one.
> You shall [not] be very industrious

And be free from all things;
You shall free the captives
And restrain the free;
You shall refresh the sick
And still take nothing for Yourself;
You shall drink the water of pain
And kindle the fire of love with the wood of virtue
Then will you live in the true desert.

(Book 1:35)

Indeed the way the desert is presented indicates that for Mechtild, as for the poet of Mengeldicht 26, to live in the desert is itself an aim, and reaching it is difficult. There is no reference to moving beyond it. The Bridegroom does not create the desert as a place of trial for his Bride, rather the desert is created by the Bride striving for a lack of attachment. For Mechtild the imaginative context of the desert is the verse from Hosea not the passage from Numbers. To live in the desert is the aim. The use of the words *niht* and *iht* in the first two lines is one which we more often associate with Eckhart, and is indicative of the extent to which his thought and the vernacular expression of it was derived from the Beguines who went before him. The word *not* is omitted from some manuscripts, which changes the sense rather radically. The state described here by Mechtild is similar to Beatrijs of Nazareth's sixth manner of loving which speaks of a freedom from the need for activity or rest.

An interesting point of comparison with these Beguine texts is the poem attributed to Eckhart, the *Granum Sinapis* (Grain of Mustard Seed).[10] The poem contains many themes familiar from the other texts discussed in this section:

The way takes you
in a wonderful wilderness
that broad and wide
stretches out immeasurably.

(IV:5–7)

the need to leave a sense of self to focus on the transcendent:

> O my soul
> go forth into God.
> Sink all my something
> into God's nothing,
> sink into the bottomless flood.

(VIII:3–5)[11]

travelling the pathless wilderness by difficult ways:

> leave place, leave time
> also avoid images.
> Go without a way
> the narrow path
> so will you arrive at the desert's track.

(VII:8–10)

For Eckhart, as for Mechtild and for the poet of Mengeldicht 26, the difficult road is the essential prelude to finding the track of the wilderness, not as in Hadewijch and the Mengeldichten 17–24 to find and follow a track through the wilderness. However, Eckhart has taken the image one step further – for him the desert is the goal because the desert is God. The stanzas describing the desert have done so as an image of the Trinity, of the unknowability of the being of God, not as an image of a life dedicated to God.

This brief analysis has shown how misleading it can be to assume that an image such as that of the desert carries a single meaning and that its use in different authors will be broadly the same. Hadewijch and the poet of Mengeldichten 17–24 are drawing on the monastic use of the image. For them the desert combines a sense of exile, anxiety and loneliness with a paradoxical sense of security and purpose as *minne* leads the poet and her audience through it – a perfect *figura* for the life they have chosen. For Mechtild and for the poet of Mengeldicht 26 the monastic context has lost its power, and for them to live in the desert is the goal. It is not created as a place of trial, rather the soul strives to create it within her by lessening her attachment to things. Eckhart on the other hand uses the vastness of the image and its featurelessness to evoke the unknowable nature of God. He associates the desert directly with the goodness of God and his being.

Without wishing to impose too rigid a developmental framework on these texts, it may be possible to posit a gradual development in the use and meaning of the image of the desert as reflected by these texts written in broadly the same spiritual milieu. In the early part of the century the image was still closely related to the *figura* of the monastic life as described by Richard of St Victor and others. It was the place of exile, trial and wandering before entry into the Promised Land. For Hadewijch and the poet of the Mengeldichten 17–24 the image of the desert as the trial endured while in exile gains its resonance from the passage in Numbers. The development from a place of trial to be left behind to a place where one aims to live is not difficult to trace. Elsewhere we have discussed the way in which for Hadewijch union with God is achieved in the midst of the experience of suffering with the humanity of Christ and a sense of exile. The transition requires a simple conflation of the place of exile where one finds the Promised Land of union with God, and the place of exile as the goal. Similarly one can follow the process by which the place of union (Mechtild) might gradually be transformed into the God with whom one is united (Eckhart).[12]

6. CONCLUSION

The effect of the papal dispensation granted to Jacques of Vitry in 1215 for the lay women to live together and to exhort one another to greater virtue and love of God was to open up, albeit briefly, a vista on to the interests and religious concerns of the laity, especially women. For men it has always been possible to satisfy a degree of religious interest by entering the Church in some capacity. The women provide us with an insight into the religious issues of the period as understood and experienced by ordinary men and women, not by the clergy. The development of the Beguine movement was part of the desire to 'democratise' religion. The desire to bring God to the people, into the market place, flowed from the dawning realisation that Christianity was properly a way of life accessible to all, not just a series of rites performed by an inner circle of initiates. There is a remarkable three-dimensional representation of the desire to bring God to the people in the cathedral in Naumburg in the former East Germany. This cathedral is famous for the sculptures of the so-called 'Naumburg Workshop', one of which is the crucifix on the rood screen. Whereas previously the crucifix would have hung suspended above the people, enabling them all to see it by looking above their heads, this life-size realistic crucifix is at about the height the actual cross would have been, only a few feet above the ground. Christ is shown in agony but smiling at his mother, and the congregation is brought right into the scene at the foot of the cross, becoming part of it. God is no longer 'out there' – he and his salvific sacrifice are a present reality for the congregation, for the ordinary people in the cathedral, almost more than for the priests on the other side of the screen.

The religious life had hitherto been carried out almost exclusively behind the walls of monasteries and convents, mostly situated outside the city. The inmates prayed for the souls of those outside the walls, but only those inside could be certain of salvation. The notion of the worthiness of a priest unleashed by Pope Gregory VII to reform the priesthood and increase ecclesiastical control over it, had as its basis the notion that a true Christian could be recognised by his way of life. It implied that the sacrament of ordination was not sufficient to make a man suitable for the office of priest, although this idea was never articulated and any pursuing it to its logical conclusion, for example by refusing to take communion if the mass was celebrated by a priest whose lifestyle they considered unworthy, were at risk from accusations of heresy by the Church. By extension the notion also implied that being a true Christian depended on your way of life and was an option open to all, outside religious life as well as within it. This proved to be a powerful force among the laity, large numbers of whom sought to live lives approximating the apostolic ideal. It is clear that it was also the motive power for the rapid growth of the Cathar heresy in Southern France, and others. Men, but especially women, began to take stock of the values underpinning their lives and those of their families. As we have seen, it was an age of increasing materialism and it seems that this fuelled the enthusiasm of some for lives of ascetic poverty. Women looked around them and considered how the wealth being so lavishly enjoyed around them had been created, and resolved to do penance as best they could for the injustices perpetrated in its acquisition. They looked at the magnificent dinners in the hall, and saw the beggars starving at the gate. Some women registered their objection to the injustice they saw around them by not eating the food paid for with what they saw as blood money.[1] Others sought to make amends for their families' sins of commission and omission by living a life as near to the apostolic ideal as they could. In many cases, as we have seen, whole families died out as husband, wife and children all embarked on the religious life. The religious life they chose was almost always that of one of the new orders, or that of a Beguine. These were all active in the cities with their growing populations, and consequently growing numbers of poor, sick and needy.

Inspired by the desire to follow the apostolic ideal of a life of service among the people, it is not surprising that the spirituality that grew out of the Beguine movement was one that required the business of everyday life in order to be practised. Because their spirituality was one of active service, those elements of mystic grace which prevented such service, or diverted attention from it, such as visions, ecstasies and trances, were dismissed as juvenile. The important part was to serve in humility. Visions and trances not only made active service difficult by interrupting activity, they also threatened humility by the risk that the Beguine so favoured would come to see herself as somehow meriting these indications of divine grace. To follow the footsteps of Christ on earth required humility to accept the rejection of one's fellow men and women. Drawing on Jesus' words to his disciples that he who would be greatest should be the servant of all, the Beguines developed a spirituality in which the central paradox was that of rejoicing in union with Christ's divinity while living in union with his suffering humanity. One of the results of this definition of *unio mystica* is that the humility of the Beguine who saw herself as the most despicable of creatures before God, doubting even that she was loved of her beloved, was transformed into the courage to stand before God and wrestle with *minne* at the most profound level.

The voices of these women and the spirituality they forged out of their circumstances have rested unheard for centuries. The voices of theology have been the male-dominated voices of the ecclesiastical hierarchies as they sought to shout each other down over the centuries since the Reformation. However, the spirituality of the Beguines did leave a legacy, the trail of which can be discerned, albeit faintly, up to the Reformation and beyond. There are two converging lines through which this inheritance was transmitted. The work of Hadewijch and other Beguines was well known to Ruusbroec and others at the monastery in Groenendael near Brussels, where most of the major Hadewijch manuscripts were preserved. When in 1379 Geert Grote drew up the rules for the community of pious lay women he had founded in Deventer and which was to develop into the movement known as the *Devotio Moderna* (the Modern Devout), he had travelled to Groenendael to meet Ruusbroec. It is impossible to be certain of the advice given to him by Ruusbroec, but it is interesting that there are certain similarities between the Modern Devout and the thought of the Beguines we have examined here. Like the early Beguines, the Modern Devouts turned their faces against the excesses of mystic phenomena such as visions, ecstasies and trances, and had a highly developed sense of service to God within society.

The other line is through the writings of the German mystic Meister Eckhart. For years seen as the founder of German mysticism, it has now been shown that Eckhart developed ideas he had gleaned from his contact with Beguines and other communities of women in his province. There are many instances when the similarities between his ideas and the expression of them and those of the Beguines are very marked. Earlier this century such similarities were seen as evidence that the Beguine texts must have been written in the fourteenth century under the influence of his teaching. Fortunately it has now been recognised that it is possible that the influence went the other way. Most recently it has been suggested that Eckhart was familiar with Marguerite Porete's condemned work *Le Mirouer des Simples Ames*. He was certainly in Paris, staying at the same place as her inquisitor at the time of her trial, and it is almost inconceivable that there would not have been discussion of the case. Posthumously condemned as a heretic in 1329, Eckhart was roundly denounced by such influential figures as the fourteenth-century mystic Ruusbroec, although Ruusbroec never mentions him by name, Jan van

Leeuwen (both resident in Groenendael) and the founder of the *Devotio Moderna* movement, Geert Grote. However, it has been shown that many of Eckhart's sermons and treatises continued to circulate anonymously in the spiritual milieu of the Modern Devout, in one case erroneously attributed to Ruusbroec himself.[2] It would seem, therefore, that, partly through the medium of anonymous distribution, Eckhart's thought continued to influence the formation of the spirituality of a movement which was to inspire many Reformation and Counter-Reformation theologians, among them Desiderius Erasmus.

The voices of these women are a valuable supplement to the sound of their male counterparts which has been dominant for so long. Increasingly people are seeking a spirituality beyond what the Church appears to offer. As in the thirteenth century they are moving away from the traditional Christian churches to other religions and forms of thought because the churches appear to be irrelevant to their concerns. The voices of these women offer an alternative Christian vision and serve to remind people that true Christianity is not a matter of form and observance, but a way of life. A life of service for others out of love for humankind and God, a life of low prestige and little public recognition. A life in which suffering, whether physical or psychological, is patiently born out of love for God, and is thereby transformed into a positive joy, not merely a martyr's crown. To increase their popularity, many churches are with some success stressing the accessibility of the love of God and the joys of community. In some cases this is stressed to the exclusion of any apparent awareness of the ontological chasm between Creator and creation. The Beguines speak rather of the awe-inspiring otherness of God, of the love that is too great to comprehend, overwhelming and totally engulfing, fearfully great. Their texts are full of the numinous, the wonder of God, and there is a profound sense of worship in their speaking. Modern church services, in their desire to make God accessible for all, sometimes seem to have stifled the consciousness of God's otherness that leads to worship. The

Beguines may provide some genuine seekers of spiritual truths
with new insights into the nature of the relationship between
God and his creation (wo)man. In other churches, people are
flocking to listen to the words of charismatic leaders. The
message of the Beguines is that unusual phenomena such
as visions, ecstatic trances and speaking in tongues are not
necessarily indicators of special grace and are certainly not in
themselves evidence of a deep spiritual life. As they and their
contemporaries were only too aware, these can be the product
of (self) delusion. The higher grace is the less dramatic one of
union with God in suffering.

The Beguine texts were written for the communities of which
the women were members. As we have seen, these communities changed over the course of the century from being small
groups of perhaps no more than half a dozen like-minded
women, to larger communities of women living in the vicinity
of Dominican houses in the cities of the Rhine and elsewhere
in Europe. The imaginary context in which their lives took
place shared many of the salient features of the courtly-love
myth of secular romance. Whereas in the courtly romance the
true lovers are repeatedly warned against believing the words
of the jealous by-standers and peasants who seek to damage
the reputation of the beloved, here the Beguines are warned
against the false teaching of those who believe there is a
simpler, less painful, way of union with God. Other voices
suggest that service is inappropriate to the brides of Christ,
and even that such union, stripped as it is of its dramatic
features, is scarcely worth striving for. To counter such false
teaching, the texts praise knightly values such as loyalty,
valour in battle, strength and endurance, and loyalty to the
beloved regardless of the lies of peasants. They also praise
the chivalric code of honourable service to a noble master or
liege-lord. But above and beyond these codes of behaviour, the
Beguines speak of the need to stand up before God, to fight
and conquer *minne*, to distrust her fickle favours as one would
those of a jade at court. Although the texts assume a hierarchy
for heaven that appears to parallel the patriarchal imperial

monarchy on earth, the theological economy presented in fact calls for considerably more independence of action and indeed courageous resistance than those theological economies traditionally presented. The community of true lovers, of *fins amans*, is under threat from false friends within and from jealous critics without. The Beguines frequently refer to the need to live harmoniously with others in community, and not to be troubled by the criticism of those who do not understand the motivation of the *fins amans*. The theology of these texts relates to the problems faced by the community because it is written to address those problems. From the Beguine texts we can clearly perceive their own awareness of the threat from outside, from those who failed to appreciate what it was that the *fins amans* were striving for and who were distrustful of their single-minded concentration on God to the virtual exclusion of the Church.

One of the features of Beguine spirituality, as we have seen, is that they were writing basically pastoral texts. There is no systematic discussion of theology, rather an emphasis on the practical living of the life of Christ. In pastoral texts theology tends to be implicit, rather than explicit. Explicitly there may even appear to be a lack of concern about theological matters, but the fundamentally theological nature of the texts can be seen in the fact that they map out the way of life under God. True theology, 'words about God', is always earthed in a context. The truths of theology may be eternal, but the language in which they are couched are necessarily dependent on time and culture. Theology must be expressed for human beings using human language and concepts. In the case of the Beguines, the truths they experienced of God are couched in the imagery of courtly love, the language of suffering and exile. There is, of course, the danger of some circularity in the argument since the theology of the text is rooted in the context in which it was written, and the context can only be deduced from the texts themselves. However, if the work is done properly then it is not so much circular as a spiral, each pass adding a further layer of understanding, a cumulative process of adding together clues; it is therefore very important that we do not set up an interpretative framework in advance which then determines how the texts are to be read. The danger of this in the case of the Beguines can be seen in the way their theology has been overlooked in favour of their literary merits, and in some cases traduced and even silenced by later concerns about heresy. The core of Christian teaching involves the concept of incarnation, and the very notion of incarnation (God made manifest in the particularities of time and place) demands that justice be done to the particularities of a text earthed in a specific historical and cultural situation (in contrast to concentrating only on reader-reaction). And justice can only be done to these particularities by recognising that they were indeed unique – no other moment in human history was or is quite the same. A proper appreciation of the Beguine texts can only be achieved through an understanding of the historical and cultural context in which they were written. The significance of the texts is not, however, limited to the time and place in which they originated. The understanding these women gained of the relationship between God and his creation (wo)man has something to say to the human condition today as well. Revelation of eternal truths about God takes place not despite the changes and chances of this life, but in and through them.

NOTES

1. THE ORIGINS AND DEVELOPMENT OF THE BEGUINE MOVEMENT

1. For discussions of attitudes to money at this time see Jacques Le Goff, *La Bourse et la Vie: Economie et Réligion au Moyen Age* (Hachette, Paris, 1986), and Lester K. Little, *Religious Poverty and the Profit Economy* (Paul Elek, London, 1978).
2. See, for example, the discussion in A. Murray, *Reason and Society in the Middle Ages* (Clarendon Press, Oxford, 1978), pp. 162–203.
3. J. Le Goff, *The Medieval Imagination* (University of Chicago Press, Chicago, 1988), p. 63; Little, *Religious Poverty*, p. 22.
4. The efforts of town councils to curb what they saw as excessive displays of wealth are described in E. Ennen, *The Medieval Woman* (Blackwell, Oxford, 1989), p. 276.
5. Le Goff, *Medieval Imagination*, p. 70.
6. For a discussion of the Gregorian reforms see, for example, R. W. Southern, *Western Society and the Church in the Middle Ages*, The Pelican History of the Church, 2 (Pelican, London, 1970). Hereafter referred to as Southern.
7. The apostolic succession reserves to those ordained either directly or indirectly by the successors of Peter and the apostles the right to take an active part in the Church and Christian salvation.
8. A more detailed discussion of the founding of these Orders can be found in Southern, pp. 240–72.
9. Another important contribution of the Order was in the area of technological advances. For interesting discussions about technological developments in the Middle Ages and their impact see, for example, Jean Gimpel, *The Medieval Machine: The Industrial Revolution of the Middle Ages*, 2nd edn (Pimlico, London, 1992) and Lynn White, Jnr, *Medieval Religion and Technology* (University of California Press, Berkeley, 1978).
10. Southern, pp. 241–2.
11. Southern, p. 242.
12. For a good discussion of the place of the poor in western society

during the Middle Ages see Michel Mollat, *The Poor in the Middle Ages: An Essay in Social History*, translated by Arthur Goldhammer (Yale University Press, New Haven, 1986).

13. Decisions on whether a preacher would be seen as a heretic or not appear to have been influenced by whether he was licensed to preach or not, and whether or not his followers were in a recognised order. Those who conformed to the demand only to preach where invited to by incumbent priests and to found an order rigorously enclosing their women followers were accepted by the Church. See Herbert Grundmann, *Religious Movements in the Middle Ages: The Historical Links between Heresy, the Mendicant Orders, and the Women's Religious Movement in the Twelfth and Thirteenth Century, with the Historical Foundations of German Mysticism*, translated by Steven Rowan (University of Notre Dame Press, Notre Dame, 1995), p. 17. Grundmann's seminal work on the Beguine movement, originally written in 1935 and revised and expanded in 1961, has only recently been translated into English. Hereafter it will be referred to as Grundmann.

14. This is discussed further in Southern, pp. 312–18.

15. Friedrich Heer, *The Medieval World: Europe from 1100 to 1350*, translated by Janet Sondheimer (Cardinal, London, 1974), p. 60.

16. Karl Bücher, *Die Frauenfrage im Mittelalter*, 2nd edn (Tübingen 1910).

17. Grundmann, p. 149.

18. See White Jnr, *Medieval Religion and Technology*, p. 16.

19. This is discussed in more detail in Grundmann, pp. 31–74.

20. A discussion of the *vita* as a polemical document can be found in Iris Geyer, *Maria von Oignies: Eine hochmittelalterliche Mystikerin zwischen Ketserei und Rechtglaübigkeit* (Peter Lang, Frankfurt am Main, 1991).

21. This point was originally made by Grundmann and more recently developed in an article by Carol Neel: Carol Neel, 'The origins of the Beguines' in *Sisters and Workers in the Middle Ages*, edited by Judith M. Bennett, Elizabeth A. Clark, Jean F. O'Barr, B. Anne Vilen, and Sarah Westphal-Wihl (University of Chicago Press, Chicago, 1989), pp. 240–60.

22. Grundmann, p. 53.

23. Grundmann, pp. 79–80.

24. Robert E. Lerner, *The Heresy of the Free Spirit in the Later Middle Ages* (University of California Press, Berkeley, 1972). Grundmann discusses the interesting possibility of a link between the followers of Amaury, who was condemned a heretic in 1210, and the heresy which came to be known as that of the Free Spirit (Grundmann, pp. 153–9). By the mid-fourteenth century the German mystic Eckhart was (erroneously) being seen as the founder of the Heresy of the Free Spirit which suggests that the connection between his spirituality

and that of the Beguines was better understood then than it has been more recently.

25. See the discussion in Grundmann pp. 78–80 and the following articles by Van Mierlo: J. van Mierlo, 'De bijnaam van Lambertus li Beges en de vroegste beteekenis van het woord begijn', *Verslagen en Mededelingen van de Koninklijke Vlaamsche Academie voor Taal- en Letterkunde* (Gent 1925), pp. 405–47; 'Lambert li Begues in verband met de oorsprong der begijnenbeweging', *Verslagen en Mededelingen van de Koninklijke Vlaamsche Academie voor Taal- en Letterkunde* (Gent 1926), pp. 1612–60; 'Ophelderingen bij de vroegste geschiedenis van het woord begijn', *Verslagen en Mededelingen van de Koninklijke Vlaamsche Academie voor Taal- en Letterkunde*(Gent 1931), pp. 983–1006.

26. An excellent detailed survey of the growth and development in one geographic area of the Beguine movement from its inception until the Reformation has been undertaken by Andreas Wilts, *Beginen im Bodenseeraum* (Thorbecke Verlag, Sigmaringen, 1994).

27. Grundmann, p. 98.

28. Grundmann, pp. 92–109.

29. The creative tension between the mystic experience of pious women and the scholastic learning of the friars, and the significant works which it produced, was first noted by Denifle and Grundmann: H. S. Denifle, 'Meister Eckeharts lateinische Schriften und die Grundanschauung seiner Lehre', *Archiv für Litteratur- und Kirchengeschichte des Mittelalters*, 2 (1886), pp. 417–652, especially Beilage II, 'Über die Anfänge der Predigtweise der deutschen Mystiker', pp. 641–52; H. Grundmann, 'Die geschichtlichen Grundlagen der Deutschen Mystik', *Deutsche Vierteljahrsschrift für Literaturwissenschaft und Geistesgeschichte, 12* (1934), pp. 400–29. It has more recently been developed in an article by John Coakley: John Coakley, 'Friars as confidants of holy women in medieval Dominican hagiography' in *Images of Sainthood in Medieval Europe*, edited by Renate Blumenfeld-Kosinski and Timea Szell (Cornell University Press, Ithaca, 1991), pp. 222–46.

30. Quoted in Southern, p. 330.

31. When in 1471 Louis XI transferred the Parisian beguinage established by Louis X in 1327 it had only two inhabitants. Karl Christ, 'La Regle des Fins Amans, eine Beginenregel aus dem ende des XIII. Jahrhunderts' in *Philologische Studien aus dem romanisch-germanischen Kulturkreise, festschrift für Karl Voretsch*, edited by B. Schadel and W. Mulertt (Max Niemeyer Verlag, Halle an der Saale, 1927), pp. 173–213, p. 175.

32. A young woman in Belgium has recently made her vows as a Beguine.

33. I am indebted to Mrs Penny Granger for doing the research which enabled me to include the following observations.

34. Norman P. Tanner, *The Church in Late Medieval Norwich 1370–1532* (Pontifical Institute of Medieval Studies, Toronto, 1984), p. 203; Roberta Gilchrist and Marilyn Oliva, *Religious Women in Medieval East Anglia*, Studies in East Anglian History 1 (Centre of East Anglian Studies, UEA, Norwich, 1993), p. 95.
35. Gilchrist and Oliva, *Religious Women*, p. 72.

2. THE LITERARY CONTEXT

1. Philip Sheldrake, *Spirituality and History: Questions of Interpretation and Method* (SPCK, London, 1991).
2. See, for example, the discomfort of academic and religious commentators with a woman such as Margery Kempe.
3. The needs of the institution may change over time, and this will be reflected in the way history is written. For a discussion of how the history of the first half of the twentieth century has influenced Hadewijch scholarship see S. Murk-Jansen, 'Hadewijch and Eckhart: Amor intellegere est' in *Eckhart and the Beguine Mystics*, edited by B. McGinn (Continuum, New York, 1995), pp. 17–30.
4. For a discussion of this point see Alcuin Blamires, *The Case for Women in Medieval Culture* (Clarendon Press, Oxford, 1997).
5. Both quotations taken from Emilie Zum Brun and Georgette Epiney-Burgard, *Woman Mystics in Medieval Europe*, translated by Sheila Hughes (Paragon House, New York, 1989), pp. 55–6.
6. For a discussion of attitudes to the Magdalene see, for example, Susan Haskins, *Mary Magdalen* (HarperCollins, London, 1994).
7. The term was first used by Nicholas Watson. For a discussion of its meaning see Nicholas Watson, 'Censorship and cultural change in late-medieval England: vernacular theology, the Oxford Translation Debate, and Arundel's Constitution of 1409', *Speculum*, 70, no. 4 (October 1995), pp. 822–64, and McGinn, 'Introduction', *Eckhart and the Beguine Mystics*, pp. 1–14.
8. An example is Hadewijch's Letter 10 which is a free translation of a text by Richard of St Victor. J. M. Schallij, 'Richard van St Victor en Hadewijch's 10e Brief', *Tijdschrift voor Nederlandse Taal- en Letterkunde*, 62 (1943), pp. 219–28.
9. Obvious contemporary examples are single working women, couples childless by choice, and homosexuals. But consider also the voices raised to argue that the contemporary myth of the superwoman has deprived men of their role, that it has left men with nowhere to stand, with nothing to do.
10. A recent biography of St Clare which deals well with her reaction to the rigorous enclosure of herself and her sisters at St Damiano is that by Marco Bartoli, *Clare of Assisi*, translated by Sister Frances Teresa osc (Darton, Longman and Todd, London, 1993).

11. One example of this is the way in which Clare of Assisi presents the enclosure of herself and her nuns as the means of enlarging their service to embrace all the mankind. Enclosure did not cut them off from the world, rather it was the means of opening up to the world: isolation as the fullness of spiritual communion.

12. This is the term Barbara Newman uses in her recent book: Barbara Newman, *From Virile Woman to Woman Christ; Studies in Medieval Religion and Literature* (University of Pennsylvania Press, Philadelphia, 1995). See for example the discussion on pp. 137 onwards.

13. Karl Christ, 'La Regle des Fins Amans, eine Beginenregel aus dem ende des XIII. Jahrhunderts' in *Philologische Studien aus dem romanisch-germanischen Kulturkreise, festschrift fur Karl Voretsch*, edited by B. Schadel and W. Mulertt (Max Niemeyer Verlag, Halle an der Saale, 1927), pp. 173–213. (Hereafter referred to as *Regle*.) I am indebted to Barbara Newman for drawing my attention to this text. She subsequently included a discussion of the text in her recent collection of essays *From Virile Woman to WomanChrist*.

14. *The Miracle of Beatrice: A Flemish Legend of c. 1300*, translated by Adriaan Barnouw (Pantheon, New York, 1944).

15. Richard of St Victor also speaks of the Queen of Sheba as the example of a soul lost in contemplation of God in his *Benjamin Minor*. See J. P. Migne (ed.), *Patrologiae Cursus Completus: Series Latinae* (Paris 1878), vol. 196, p. 181.

16. *Regle*, p. 201.

17. *Regle*, p. 204.

18. Translation from F. Zum Brunn and G. Epinay-Burgard, *Women Mystics in Medieval Europe*, translated from the French by Sheila Hughes (Paragon House, New York, 1939), p. 164.

19. Hadewijch translations, with my own modifications, are taken from *Hadewijch, The Complete Works,* translated by Mother Columba Hart, Classics of Western Spirituality (SPCK, London, 1980). Where the texts are not included in Hart, the translations are my own. The page reference in Hart is given only for prose texts.

20. For a more detailed discussion of the arguments see S. Murk-Jansen, 'The mystic theology of the thirteenth-century mystic, Hadewijch, and its literary expression', *The Medieval Mystical Tradition in England*, V (1992), edited by Marion Glasscoe (Boydell and Brewer, Cambridge, 1991), pp. 117–27.

21. See for example the discussion in 1 John 4.

22. Zum Brunn, p. 91.

23. There is good biblical support for this: 'It is a fearful thing to fall into the hands of the living God' (Hebrews 10:31) and 'For the Lord thy God is a consuming fire, even a jealous God' (Deuteronomy 4:24).

24. This insight that trinitarian language is the way in which the aspects of God are made known and comprehensible to humankind, is not unique to Hadewijch (one of the points against Eckhart was that he

denied the differentiation between the persons of the Trinity in the innermost being of God).

25. This was to prove problematical for Eckhart early in the fourteenth century.

3. FOUR LIVES: FOUR TEXTS

1. See Hadewijch II below.
2. Further discussion of Beatrijs, *vita*, her life and work can be found in Roger De Ganck, *Beatrijs of Nazareth in her Context*, 3 vols (Cistercian Publications, Kalamazoo, 1991).
3. Kurt Ruh, *Geschichte der abendländischen Mystik*, 4 vols (C. H. Beck, Munich, 1993), vol. 2, pp. 144–5. Hereafter referred to as Ruh.
4. Ruh, vol. 2, p. 145.
5. Beatrijs van Nazareth, *Van Seuen Manieren van Heileger Minnen*, edited by H. W. J. Vekeman and J. J. Th. M. Tersteeg (N. V. W. J. Thieme & Cie, Zutphen, 1970), p. 35. Hereafter referred to as *Vekeman*. The translations are my own.
6. *Vekeman*, p. 36.
7. *Vekeman*, p. 39.
8. *Vekeman*, p. 41.
9. The concern to distinguish the one from the other, the one heretical and the other not, is of a later date and has obscured the debate concerning the date and authorship of many texts, among them texts in the Hadewijch manuscripts such as the Mengeldichten 17–24.
10. *Vekeman*, p. 43.
11. *Vekeman*, p. 48.
12. *Vekeman*, p. 52.
13. *Vekeman*, p. 51.
14. *Vekeman*, p. 56.
15. In this context it is interesting to note that in her 'List of the Perfect Ones' Hadewijch refers to one 'Beatrijs' which suggests that they may have known of each other.
16. One of these suffered a direct hit during the Second World War and is now a war memorial, the other is still standing intact.
17. For discussions and examples of early Cistercian spirituality see: Caroline Walker Bynum, *Jesus as Mother: Studies in the Spirituality of the High Middle Ages* (University of California Press, Berkeley, 1982), and *Ein Lied, das nur die Liebe lehrt: Texte des Frühen Zisterzienser Mönche*, edited by Gertrude and Thomas Sartory (Herderbücherei, Frieburg, 1981).
18. The definite article *Das*, 'The', at the beginning of the title is a later insertion which subtly changes the meaning. Fortunately the trend in modern scholarship is now to leave it out.
19. For further discussion and references see Ruh, p. 251.

20. This is in marked contrast to the unmoved Bridegroom of Bernard's commentaries.
21. *Fliessende Licht der Gottheit*, Chapter 4:12.
22. See below, Hadewijch II. For a summary of the discussion concerning the authorship of Letter 28 see Ruh, vol. 2, pp. 212, 225–30. The uncertainty concerning the authorship of some of the texts in the Hadewijch manuscripts may be an indication that the texts were first collected together after the author's death. Whether or not the letter is properly attributed to Hadewijch, it is of interest that the compiler of the manuscript thought it of sufficient importance to include it. I have argued elsewhere that the letter's position in the collection should perhaps be seen as an illustration of the theme of *vercrighen in ontbliuen*, 'to obtain within the experience of lack', which is so central to Hadewijch's mystic theology. S. Murk-Jansen, *The Measure of Mystic Thought*, pp. 111–12.
23. One of the perfect she lists is a Beguine 'whom Master Robert had killed on account of her veritable love'. It seems likely that this 'Master Robert' was Robert Le Bougre who was active in the Inquisition in Flanders during the 1230s and the Beguine has been identified with Aelais whom he had burnt at the stake in 1236. Hadewijch also mentions hermits living on the walls of Jerusalem. Jerusalem finally fell to the Khoresmians on 23 August 1244 and there will have been no Christian hermits living in or around Jerusalem after that date.
24. The most detailed study of the likely influences on Hadewijch's imagery is Joris Reynaert, *De Beeldspraak van Hadewijch* (Lanoo, Tielt, 1981). There is also a discussion of the probable influences on her mystic thinking in Paul Mommaers, *Hadewijch, Schrijfster, Begijn, Mystica* (Attiora, Averbode, 1989).
25. Ruh, vol. 2, p. 163.
26. Ruh, vol. 2, p. 225.
27. Grundmann, p. 98.
28. I discuss the effects of this gender reversal elsewhere. S. Murk-Jansen, 'The use of gender and gender-related imagery in Hadewijch' in *Gender and Text in the Later Middle Ages*, edited by Jane Chance (University Press of Florida, Gainesville, 1996), pp. 52–68.
29. For a good discussion of the concept of 'unfaith' in Hadewijch see chapter 3 in Bernie McGinn, *The Flowering of Mysticism*, vol. 3 of *The Presence of God: A History of Western Christian Mysticism* (Continuum, New York, forthcoming). I would like to thank Professor McGinn for sending me a copy of a draft of this chapter.
30. She speaks for example of becoming all that *minne* is, and how in union with *minne* (wo)man becomes God (Letter 30:167–8, Hart, p. 119, Letter 17:89–99, Hart, p. 84).
31. The arguments are discussed in detail in S. Murk-Jansen, *The*

Measure of Mystic Thought, Göppinger Arbeiten zur Germanistik 536 (Kümmerle Verlag, Göppingen, 1991).

32. However this has recently been disputed. See Mary A. Suydam, 'The politics of authorship: Hadewijch of Antwerp and the Mengeldichten', *Mystics Quarterly*, 22 (1996), pp. 2–20.

33. A. C. Bouman, 'Die literarische Stellung der Dichterin Hadewijch', *Neophilogus*, 8 (1923), pp. 270–9. The suggested influence of Eckhart on Hadewijch was vigorously refuted by Van Mierlo in an article later that same year. J. van Mierlo, 'Hadewijch en Eckhart', *Dietse Warande en Belfort* (1923), pp. 1138–55. For a discussion of both articles see S. Murk-Jansen, 'Hadewijch and Eckhart: Amor intellegere est', *Meister Eckhart and the Beguine Mystics*, pp. 17–30.

34. See R. Lievens, 'Een nieuw Mengeldicht uit de School van Hadewijch', *Leuvense Bijdragen*, 47 (1958), pp. 65–85; S. Murk-Jansen, 'An anonymous mystic text of the thirteenth century', *Canadian Journal of Netherlandic Studies*, 11, no. 2 (1990), pp. 11–18; S. Murk-Jansen, *The Measure of Mystic Thought*, pp. 40–4.

35. This insistence on the loss of individual will is subsequently taken up by Eckhart in his insistence on the absolute poverty of the soul – a poverty so complete that the soul does not even have a will with which to desire the divine will. See Eckhart's sermon, *Beati pauperes spiritu* in *Meister Eckhart Sermons and Treatises*, translated and edited by M. O'C. Walshe, 3 vols (Element, Shaftesbury, 1990), Sermon 87, vol. 2, pp. 269–77.

36. *Le Mirouer des Simples Ames*, edited by Romana Guarnieri, Corpus Christianorum Continuatio Medievalis LXIX (Brepols, Turnhout, 1986), chapter 38, p. 122.

37. *Fliessende Licht der Gottheit*, Book 1:44.

4. THE BEGUINES AND THE CHURCH

1. Kurt Ruh, 'Mechtild von Magdeburg und Wichmann von Arnstein', *Zeitschrift für deutsche Altertum*, 120 (1991), pp. 322–5.

2. For further details see Ruh, vol. 2, p. 288.

3. In the following section I have drawn extensively on the work of John Coakley. John Coakley, 'Friars as confidants of holy women' in *Images of Sainthood in Medieval Europe*, edited by Renate Blumenfeld-Kosinski and Timea Szell (Cornell University Press, Ithaca, 1991), pp. 222–46.

4. Coakley, 'Friars as confidants', p. 246.

5. BRIDES IN THE DESERT: KEY IMAGES IN BEGUINE SPIRITUALITY

1. The correct translation of the German *husvrouwe* is 'lady of the house' or 'chatelaine' not 'housewife' as some translations would have it!

2. See for example Poem in Stanzas 39.
3. The translations of Mechtild's work are taken, with only minor alterations, from Mechtild of Magdeburg, *Flowing Light of the Godhead*, translated by C. M. Galvani, edited by S. Clark (Garland, New York, 1991).
4. Christina of Markyate, a hermit and later nun near St Albans in the twelfth century, tells how she was plagued by almost overwhelming feelings of sexual desire for her priest until at last Christ vouchsafed her a vision in which she cradled him in her arms as a baby. Thereafter she was not again troubled by lust. *The Life of Christina of Markyate*, edited and translated by C. H. Talbot (Clarendon, Oxford, 1959).
5. A good recent study of attitudes to childhood during this period is Shulamith Shahar, *Childhood in the Middle Ages* (Routledge, London, 1990).
6. See for example Book 7:65; Clark (ed.) and Galvani (tr.), *Flowing Light*, pp. 269–70.
7. The willingness to postpone entry into heaven, or even to give it up entirely, for love of God is a theme the Beguines return to frequently. It illustrates the extent of their love for God and also the degree to which their will has become one with the will of God. Another example occurs in the poem found in a manuscript of 1351. S. Murk-Jansen, 'An anonymous mystic text of the thirteenth century', p. 14.
8. Annemarie Schimmel, *As Through a Veil: Mystical Poetry in Islam* (Columbia University Press, New York, 1982). This book on the mystical poets of Islam contains insights into the creation of mystical poetry which are equally applicable to Christian texts.
9. A note on the translations: the Middle Dutch word *wuestine* and the Middle High German word *wuste*, can mean both desert and wilderness. I have used both interchangeably.
10. An interesting discussion of this poem as well as a translation of the text into modern German can be found in Kurt Ruh, *Meister Eckhart: Theologe Prediger Mystiker* (C. H. Beck, Munich, 1985), pp. 47–59.
11. Note the similarity to Mechtild of Magdeburg's description of the need to lose the something of self and sink into the nothing of God.
12. With this schematic development in mind, it is clear that the poet of the Mengeldichten 17–24 was writing in context much closer to that of Hadewijch than that of Mechtild, or even of the poet of Mengeldicht 26. No single piece of evidence of this kind is conclusive, but it is another indication that we are dealing with texts generated in the same milieu at the same time and arguably by the same author. The question of the Mengeldichten 25–29 is more difficult. The parallel between Mengeldicht 25 and the text by Mechtild of Magdeburg supports the hypothesis that these poems reflect Beguine spirituality of the second half of the thirteenth century rather than the first.

6. CONCLUSION

1. One of the most significant works discussing the ways in which women may have used food as a means of protest in the Middle Ages is Caroline Walker Bynum, *Holy Feast and Holy Fast: The Religious Significance of Food to Medieval Women* (University of California Press, Berkeley, 1987).

2. See R. A. Ubbink, *De Receptie van Meister Eckhart in de Nederlanden gedurende de Middeleeuwen*, PhD thesis at the University of Leiden in 1978 (Rodopi, Amsterdam, 1978); and also my article in which I draw substantially on Ubbink's research in order to make it more widely known to an English audience: S. Murk-Jansen, 'The apocryphal followers of Eckhart' in *The Eckhart Review* (Spring 1998).

SELECTED BIBLIOGRAPHY

TEXT EDITIONS

Beatrijs van Nazareth, *Beatrijs van Nazareth Van Seuen Manieren van Heileger Minnen*, ed. H. W. J. Vekeman and J. J. Th. M. Tersteeg (N. V. W. J. Thieme & Cie, Zutphen, 1970).

Cistercians, *Ein Lied, das nur die Liebe lehrt: Texte des Frühen Zisterzienser Mönche*, ed. Gertrude and Thomas Sartory (Herderbücherei, Frieburg, 1981).

Eckhart, *Meister Eckhart Sermons and Treatises* (3 vols), tr. and ed. M. O'C. Walshe (Element, Shaftesbury, 1990).

Hadewijch, *Hadewijch: The Complete Works*, tr. Mother Columba Hart, Classics of Western Spirituality (SPCK, London, 1980).

Mechtild of Magdeburg, *Flowing Light of the Godhead*, tr. C. M. Galvani, ed. S. Clark (Garland, New York, 1991).

Christina of Markyate, *The Life of Christina of Markyate*, ed. and tr. C. H. Talbot (Clarendon Press, Oxford, 1959).

Marguerite Porete, *Le Mirouer des Simples Ames*, ed. Romana Guarnieri, Corpus Christianorum Continuatio Medievalis LXIX (Brepols, Turnhout, 1986).

Bardoel, A. A., 'Hadewijch of Brabant and the hermeneutics of desire', *Dutch Crossing*, 32 (August 1987), pp. 26–36.

Bardoel, A. A., 'The psychology of vision in Hadewijch', *Mystics Quarterly*, XVII, no. 2 (June 1991), pp. 79–93.

Bartoli, M., *Clare of Assisi*, tr. Sister Frances Teresa OSC (Darton, Longman and Todd, London, 1993).

Blamires, A., *The Case for Women in Medieval Culture* (Clarendon Press, Oxford, 1997).

Bolton, B. M., 'Some thirteenth century women in the Low Countries: a special case?', *Nederlands Archief voor Kerkgeschiedenis*, 61 (1981), pp. 7–29.

Bouman, A. C., 'Die literarische Stellung der Dichterin Hadewijch', *Neophilologus*, 8 (1923), pp. 270–9.

Bowie, Fiona (ed.), *Beguine Spirituality* (SPCK, London, 1989).

Brandsma, T., 'Wanneer schreef Hadewijch hare visioenen?', *Studia Catholica*, 2 (1926), pp. 238–56.

Bücher, Karl, *Die Frauenfrage im Mittelalter*, 2nd edn (Tübingen 1910).

Butler, Dom Cuthbert, *Western Mysticism*, 3rd edn (Constable, London, 1967).

Bynum, C. W., *Jesus as Mother: Studies in the Spirituality of the High Middle Ages* (University of California Press, Berkeley, 1982).

Bynum, C. W., 'Women mystics and eucharistic devotion in the thirteenth century', *Women's Studies*, 11 (1984), pp. 179–214.

Bynum, C. W., *Holy Feast and Holy Fast: The Religious Significance of Food to Medieval Women* (University of California Press, Berkeley, 1987).

Bynum, C. W., *Fragmentation and Redemption: Essays on Gender and the Human Body in Medieval Religion* (Zone Books, New York, 1991).

Chenu, M. D., *Nature, Man, and Society in the Twelfth Century: Essays on New Theological Perspectives in the Latin West* (University of Chicago Press, Chicago, 1968).

Christ, K., 'La Regle des Fins Amans, eine Beginenregel aus dem ende des XIII. Jahrhunderts' in *Philologische Studien aus dem romanisch-germanischen Kulturkreise, festschrift für Karl Voretsch*, ed. B. Schadel and W. Mulertt (Max Niemeyer Verlag, Halle an der Saale, 1927), pp. 173–213.

Coakley, J., 'Friars as confidants of holy women in medieval Dominican hagiography', *Images of Sainthood in Medieval Europe*, ed. Renate Blumenfeld-Kosinski and Timea Szell (Cornell University Press, Ithaca, 1991), pp. 222–46.

DeGanck, R., *Beatrice of Nazareth in her Context*, 3 vols (Cistercian Publications, Kalamazoo, 1991).

Denifle, H. S., 'Meister Eckeharts lateinische Schriften und die Grundanschauung seiner Lehre', *Archiv für Litteratur-und Kirchengeschichte des Mittelalters*, 2 (1886), pp. 417–652.

Dinzelbacher P. and D. R. Bauer (eds), *Frauenmystik im Mittelalter* (Weingarten 1984).

Dinzelbacher, P. and D. R. Bauer (eds), *Religiöse Frauenbewegungen und mystische Frömmigkeit im Mittelalter* (Böhlau Verlag, Cologne, 1988).

Dronke, P., *Women Writers of the Middle Ages: A Critical Study of Texts from Perpetua (+203) to Marguerite Porete (+1310)* (Cambridge University Press, Cambridge, 1984).

Duby, G., *Le Chevalier, la Femme et le Prêtre* (Paris 1981).

Ennen, E., *The Medieval Woman* (Blackwell, Oxford, 1989).

Epiney-Burgard, G. and Zum Brunn, E., *Women Mystics in Medieval Europe* (Paragon Press, New York, 1989).

Geyer, I., *Maria von Oignies: Eine hochmittelalterliche Mystikerin zwischen Ketserei und Rechtglaübigkeit* (Peter Lang, Frankfurt am Main, 1991).

Gilchrist, R. and Oliva, M., *Religious Women in Medieval East Anglia*,

Studies in East Anglian History 1 (Centre of East Anglian Studies, UEA, Norwich, 1993).

Gilson, E., *The Spirit of Medieval Philosophy* (London 1936).

Gimpel, J., *The Medieval Machine: The Industrial Revolution of the Middle Ages*, 2nd edn (Pimlico, London, 1992).

Gooday, Francis, 'Mechthild of Magdeburg and Hadewijch of Antwerp: a comparison', *Ons Geestelijk Erf*, 48 (1974), pp. 305–62.

Grübel, I., *Bettelorden und Frauenfrömmigkeit: Das Verhältnis der Mendikanten zu Nonnenklöstern und Beginen am Beispiel Strassburg und Basel*, Kulturgeschichtliche Forschungen, 9 (Munich 1987).

Grundmann, H., 'Die geschichtlichen Grundlagen der Deutschen Mystik', *Deutsche Vierteljahrsschrift für Literaturwissenschaft und Geistesgeschichte*, 12 (1934), pp. 400–29.

Grundmann, H., *Religiöse Bewegungen im Mittelalter*, 2nd edn (Hildesheim 1961).

Grundmann, H., *Religious Movements in the Middle Ages: The Historical Links between Heresy, the Mendicant Orders, and the Women's Religious Movement in the Twelfth and Thirteenth Century, with the Historical Foundations of German Mysticism*, tr. Steven Rowan (University of Notre Dame Press, Notre Dame, 1995).

Guest, T., *Some Aspects of Hadewijch's Poetic Form in the Strofische Gedichten* (Martinus Nijhoff, The Hague, 1975).

Haskins, S., *Mary Magdalen* (HarperCollins, London, 1994).

Heer, F., *The Medieval World: Europe from 1100 to 1350*, tr. Janet Sondheimer (Cardinal, London, 1974).

Hendrix, G., 'Hadewijch benaderd vanuit de tekst over de 22ste Volmaakte?', *Leuvense Bijdragen*, 65 (1978), pp. 129–45.

Inge, W. R., *Christian Mysticism* (London 1899).

Labarge, Margaret Wade, *A Small Sound of the Trumpet: Women in Medieval Life* (Beacon Press, Boston, 1986).

Le Goff, J., *Time, Work and Culture in the Middle Ages* (University of Chicago Press, Chicago, 1980).

Le Goff, J., *La Bourse et la Vie. Economie et Réligion au Moyen Age*, Textes du XXe Siècle (Hachette, Paris, 1986).

Le Goff, J., *The Medieval Imagination* (University of Chicago Press, Chicago, 1988).

Leclercq, J., 'The renewal of theology' in *Renaissance and Renewal in the Twelfth Century*, ed. R. L. Benson and G. Constable (Clarendon Press, Oxford, 1982), pp. 68–87.

Leclercq, J., *The Love of Learning and the Desire for God: A Study of Monastic Culture* (Fordham University Press, New York, 1982).

Leguay, J.-P., *La Rue au Moyen Age* (Ouest France, Rennes, 1984).

Lerner, R. E., *The Heresy of the Free Spirit in the Later Middle Ages* (University of California Press, Berkeley, 1972).

Lewis, Gertrud Jaron, Willaert, Frank and Govers, Marie-José, *Bibliographie zur deutschen Frauenmystik des Mittelalters Mit einem Anhang zu Beatrijs van Nazareth und Hadewijch* (Erich Schmidt Verlag, Berlin, 1989).

Lievens, R., 'Een nieuw Mengeldicht uit de School van Hadewijch', *Leuvense Bijdragen*, 47 (1958), pp. 65–85.

Little, L. K., *Religious Poverty and the Profit Economy in Medieval Europe* (Paul Elek, London, 1978).

Louth, A., *The Origins of the Christian Mystical Tradition: From Plato to Denys* (Blackwell, Oxford, 1981).

Lucas, Elona K., 'Psychological and spiritual growth in Hadewijch and Julian of Norwich', *Studia Mystica*, IX (1986), pp. 3–20.

McDonnell, E. W., *The Beguines and Beghards in Medieval Culture: With Special Emphasis on the Belgian Scene* (New Brunswick 1954).

McGinn, B. (ed.), *Eckhart and the Beguine Mystics* (Continuum, New York, 1995).

McGinn, B., 'The changing shape of late medieval mysticism', *Church History*, 65 (1996), pp. 197–219.

McGinn, B., *The Flowering of Mysticism*, vol. 3 of *The Presence of God: A History of Western Christian Mysticism* (Continuum, New York, forthcoming).

Mierlo, J. van, 'Hadewijch en Eckhart', *Dietse Warande en Belfort* (1923), pp. 1138–55.

Mierlo, J. van, 'De bijnaam van Lambertus li Beges en de vroegste beteekenis van het woord begijn', *Verslagen en Mededelingen van de Koninklijke Vlaamsche Academie voor Taal- en Letterkunde* (Gent 1925), pg. 405–47.

Mierlo, J. van, 'Lambert li Begues in verband met de oorsprong der begijnenbeweging', *Verslagen en Mededelingen van de Koninklijke Vlaamsche Academie voor Taal- en Letterkunde* (Gent 1926), pp. 612–60.

Mierlo, J. van, 'Ophelderingen bij de vroegste geschiedenis van het woord begijn', *Verslagen en Mededelingen van de Koninklijke Vlaamsche Academie voor Taal- en Letterkunde* (Gent 1931), pp. 983–1006.

Mierlo, J. van, 'Hadewijch en Willem van St. Thierry', *Ons Geestelijk Erf*, 3 (1929), pp. 45–59.

Migne, J. P. (ed.), *Patrologiae Cursus Completus: Series Latina*, 221 vols (Paris 1878).

Mollat, M., *The Poor in the Middle Ages: An Essay in Social History*, tr. Arthur Goldhammer (Yale University Press, New Haven, 1986).

Mommaers, P., *Hadewijch: Schrijfster-Begijn-Mystica*, Cahiers voor levensverdieping (Attiora, Averbode, 1989).

Murk-Jansen, S., 'An anonymous mystic text of the thirteenth century', *Canadian Journal of Netherlandic Studies*, 11, no. 2 (Autumn 1990), pp. 11–18.

Murk-Jansen, S., *The Measure of Mystic Thought: A Study of Hadewijch's Mengeldichten*, Göppinger Arbeiten zur Germanistik, 536 (Kümmerle Verlag, Göppingen, 1991).

Murk-Jansen, S., 'The mystic theology of the thirteenth-century mystic,

Hadewijch, and its literary expression'. *The Medieval Mystical Tradition in England*, V (1992), ed. Marion Glasscoe (Boydell and Brewer, Cambridge, 1992), pp. 117–27.

Murk-Jansen, S., 'Hadewijch and Eckhart: Amor intellegere est' in *Eckhart and the Beguine Mystics*, ed. B. McGinn (Continuum, New York, 1995), pp. 17–30.

Murk-Jansen, S., 'The use of gender and gender-related imagery in Hadewijch', *Gender and Text in the Later Middle Ages*, ed. Jane Chance (University Press of Florida, Gainesville, 1996), pp. 52–68.

Murk-Jansen, S., 'The Apocryphal Followers of Meister Eckhart?', *The Eckhart Review* (Spring 1998).

Murray, A., *Reason and Society in the Middle Ages* (Clarendon Press, Oxford, 1978).

Neel, C., 'The origins of the Beguines', *Sisters and Workers in the Middle Ages*, ed. J. M. Bennet, E. A. Clark, J. F. O'Barr, B. A. Vilen and S. Westphal-Wihl (University of Chicago Press, Chicago, 1989), pp. 240–60.

Newman, B., *From Virile Woman to WomanChrist; Studies in Medieval Religion and Literature* (University of Pennsylvania Press, Philadelphia, 1995).

Paepe, N. de, *Hadewijch Strofische Gedichten: Een Studie van de Minne in het Kader der 12e en 13e eeuwse Mystiek en Profane Minnelyriek* (Koninklijke Vlaamse Academie voor Taal- en Letterkunde, Ghent, 1967).

Pernoud, Régine, *La Femme au Temps des Cathédrales* (Hachette, Paris, 1980).

Reynaert, J., *De Beeldspraak van Hadewijch* (Lanoo, Tielt, 1981).

Reypens, L., 'Een nieuw Hadewijch-handschrift', *Ons Geestelijk Erf*, 37 (1963), pp. 344–5.

Ruh, Kurt, 'Beginenmystik: Hadewijch, Mechthild von Magdeburg, Marguerite Porete', *Zeitschrift für deutsches Altertum und deutsche Literatur*, 106 (1977), pp. 265–77.

Ruh, Kurt, *Meister Eckhart: Theologe Prediger Mystiker* (C. H. Beck, Munich, 1985).

Ruh, Kurt, *Geschichte der abendländischen Mystik*, 4 vols (C. H. Beck, Munich, 1993).

Ruh, Kurt, 'Mechtild von Magdeburg und Wichmann von Arnstein', *Zeitschrift für deutsches Altertum*, 120 (1991), pp. 322–5.

Schallij, J. M., 'Richard van St Victor en Hadewijch's 10e Brief', *Tijdschrift voor Nederlandse Taal- en Letterkunde*, 62 (1943), pp. 219–28.

Schimmel, A., *As Through a Veil: Mystical Poetry in Islam* (Columbia University Press, New York, 1982).

Shahar, S., *Childhood in the Middle Ages* (Routledge, London, 1990).

Sheldrake, P., *Spirituality and History: Questions of Interpretation and Method* (SPCK, London, 1991).

Smalley, B., *The Study of the Bible in the Middle Ages* (Blackwell, Oxford, 1952).

Southern, R. W., *Western Society and the Church in the Middle Ages*, The Pelican History of the Church (Pelican, London, 1970).

Suydam, M. A., 'The politics of authorship: Hadewijch of Antwerp and the Mengeldichten', *Mystics Quarterly*, 22 (1996), pp. 2–20.

Tanner, N. P., *The Church in Late Medieval Norwich 1370–1532* (Pontifical Institute of Medieval Studies, Toronto, 1984).

Ubbink, R. A., *De Receptie van Meister Eckhart in de Nederlanden gedurende de Middeleeuwen*, PhD thesis at the University of Leiden (Rodopi, Amsterdam, 1978).

Underhill, E., *Mysticism* (reprinted Meridian, New York, 1960).

Verdeyen, P., 'Over de Auteur van Mengeldichten 17 to 24' in *Hoofsheid en Devotie*, ed. J. D. Janssens (Brussels 1982), pp. 147–55.

Watson, N., 'Censorship and cultural change in late-medieval England: vernacular theology, the Oxford Translation Debate, and Arundel's Constitution of 1409', *Speculum*, 70, no. 4 (October 1995), pp. 822–64.

White Jnr, L., *Medieval Religion and Technology* (University of California Press, Berkeley, 1978).

Willaert, F., 'Hadewijch en Maria Magdalena' in *Opstellen voor Dr Jan Deschamps*, ed. Cockx-Indestege and F. Hendrickx, Miscellanea Neerlandica, I-II, 2 vols (Leuven 1987), II, pp. 57–69.

Wilson, K. M. (ed.), *Medieval Women Writers* (Athens Georgia 1984).

Wilts, A., *Beginen im Bodenseeraum* (Thorbecke Verlag, Sigmaringen, 1994).

Zeyde, M. H. van der, *Hadewijch, een Studie over de Mens en de Schrijfster* (Den Haag 1934).